# Tuscany

APA PUBLICATIONS

VIENNA
Salzburg
AUSTRIA
Geneva
L. Leman
Lausanne
Montreux
Interlaken
Schwyz
LIECHTEN-STEIN
Wildspitze
Innsbruck
Grossglockner
Annecy
Mt. Blanc
4807 m
M. Rosa
4634 m
SWITZERLAND
P. Bernina
4049 m
3772 m
Brenner
3797 m
Graz
Grenoble
Aosta
Locarno
Lugano
ALTO ADIGE
Lienz
Plöckenpass
Klagenfurt
Mt. Pelvoux
4103 m
L. Maggiore
L. di Como
Como
Bolzano
(Bozen)
Villach
Loibelpass
M. Viso
3841m
Torino
(Turin)
Novara
MILANO
(Milan)
Bergamo
Trento
Pordenone
Udine
Ljubljana
Zagreb
PIEDMONTE
Alessandria
L. di Garda
Verona
SLOVENIA
CROATIA
Cuneo
Piacenza
Mantua
Padua
Trieste
FRANCE
Savona
Genova
(Genoa)
Parma
Po
Venezia
(Venice)
Rijeka
Karlovac
Grasse
MONACO
EMILIA-ROMAGNA
Modena
Ferrara
Chioggia
Cannes
Nice
San Remo
La Spezia
Bologna
Ravenna
Pula
Banja Luka
Ligurian Sea
Pisa
Livorno
Firenze
(Florence)
Bellaria
Rimini
SAN MARINO
Zadar
BOSNIA-
HERZEGOVINA
TUSCANY
Arezzo
Split
ELBA
Siena
M. Amiata
1738 m
Pescara
Bastia
Corte
Grosseto
ITALY
Perugia
Adriatic Sea
Maribor
Ajaccio
CORSE
(CORSICA)
Viterbo
Terni
Gr. Sasso
D'Italia
2914 m
Ancona
Dubrovnik
Bonifacio
Civitavecchia
LATIO
L'Aquila
Porto Torres
Olbia
ROMA
(Rome)
Latina
ABRUZZO
S. Severo
Vieste
Oristano
SARDEGNA
(SARDINIA)
ISOLE
PONZIANE
Napoli
(Naples)
Vesuvius
1277 m
Foggia
Bari
Iglesias
Cagliari
Salerno
CAMPANIA
Potenza
PUGLI
Brindisi
Taranto
Lecce
The Tyrrhenian Sea
CALABRIA
Cosenza
Mediterranean Sea
Crotone
AEOLIAN ISLANDS
Catanzaro
Trapani
Palermo
Messina
Reggio di Calábria
Bizerte
Marsala
M. Etna
3323 m
TUNIS
Caltanissetta
Catania
J. Serj
1357 m
Nabeul
Agrigento
SICILIA
(SICILY)
Gela
Siracusa
Ionian Sea
Sousse
Kairouan
TUNISIA
MALTA
Valletta
Sfax
Sicily and Italy
125 miles / 200 km

# Welcome!

From the glorious cities of Florence and Siena to the leaning Tower of Pisa, the castles of Chianti and the caves of Garfagnana, Tuscany boasts many of Italy's blockbuster sights. It also has some of its loveliest scenery; the rolling Tuscan hills, with their vineyards, olive groves and ochre-coloured villages, have enchanted foreign visitors for centuries, persuading many of them to buy and renovate an old farmhouse or *palazzo* and extend their stay.

In these pages, Insight Guides' corespondent in Florence, Silvia Brunelli, has distilled the best of Tuscany in 14 itineraries, seven of them based on Florence and seven on the Tuscany region, each with ideas on eating out and accommodation. Supporting the itineraries are sections on history and culture, Tuscan cuisine and shopping in Florence; at the back of the book is a practical information section with tips on everything from getting around and money matters to accommodation.

 **Silvia Brunelli** was born in Florence. Though she soon moved away, she returned later, first as a student to study history of art and then to work as a writer and translator. In this book, Silvia's aim was to shed the aloofness for which Tuscans are famous and share the many pleasures and quiet corners of Tuscany that she and her friends have discovered over the years.

C O N T E N T S

## History & Culture

From the Etruscans and Romans to the Medici and the Renaissance – an introduction to the events and forces that have shaped Tuscany's rich history and culture ......................................................**10**

## Itineraries

**These 14 tours link the highlights of Tuscany. The first seven are based on Florence and Fiesole. The remaining tours cover the rest of the region.**

### FLORENCE



*Pages 2/3:*
*The Tuscan*
*hills*

## Eating Out and Shopping



## Practical Information



## Maps

*Pages 8/9:*
*Monte dei Paschi*
*di Siena*

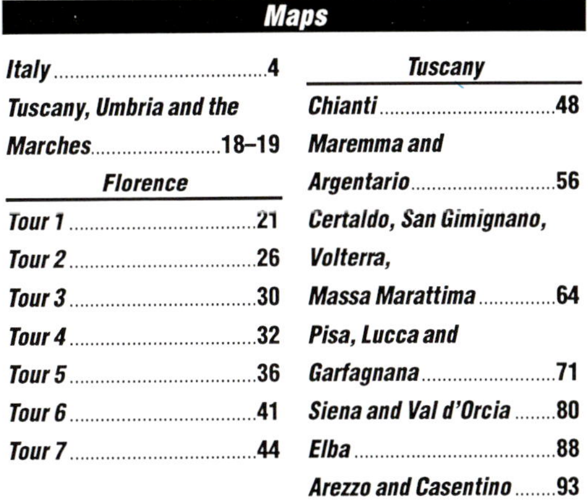

# HISTORY

$T$uscany has always succeeded in preserving its intellectual unity – even when the region was fragmented or forced to give up its independence. In a sense Tuscany's past is an inseparable part of its present. Although this does give it dignity, it also constitutes a burden, with which it is not easy to live.

Florence is about 2,000 years old, but unlike Rome or other Italian cities it has no mythic origins. Toward the end of the 10th century BC, the Villanovans settled in the exact spot where the centre of the city is located today. In the 7th century BC, the Etruscans settled in the hills surrounding Florence. It is the Etruscans to

*Palazzo Pitti and Forte di Belvedere*

whom Tuscany owes its first political institutions and the first land utilisation. While remaining a loose association of free cities without becoming a unified state, the Etruscans nevertheless developed a strong sense of solidarity and unity. The Etruscan settlements included Roselle, Chiusi, Fiesole, Bolsena, Populonia and Volterra. Within three centuries, however, the Etruscans had been absorbed into new Roman settlements, sometimes forced to do so if they did not join willingly.

During the 1st century BC the Romans founded a colony on the swampy uninviting plain, below Fiesole, giving it the name 'Florentia'. Even today, the centre of Florence is still located on the exact site of that rectangularly designed city, with even the network of streets following those laid out by

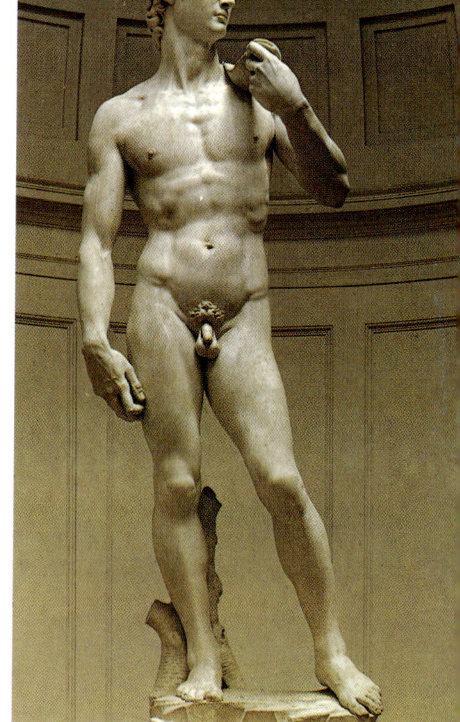
*Michelangelo's David*

the Romans. Florentia was a centre of trade. During the 3rd century AD, the city acquired a cosmopolitan character as it attracted merchants and artisans from the East. Christianity was introduced by a Greek named Mynias. Florentia then, under Constantine, became a diocesan town, but the new faith was very slow in spreading.

During the 5th century AD a depression set in which was to last for 500 years. Little is known about the history of the region during the death throes of the Roman Empire. It was, however, ravaged by the Ostrogoths. Even Florence was destroyed and then conquered by the Byzantines and Lombards (from 568 to 774).

None of the Ostrogoths, Byzantines, Lombards or Carolingians, nor even Italy's feudal kings, left substantial traces. Visible evidence

*Florence in 1480*

of the rediscovery of Roman ideas has been found in the form of the first ring of walls encircling the city – dating to the 6th century and replicating the outline of the original Roman forum.

From the 11th century, Florence grew so fast that the city required a second ring of walls crossing the Arno, making the river an important trade artery. A tremendous flurry of building activity transformed the city into a mediaeval Manhattan with over 150 towers. This was followed by the construction of most of the churches (S Miniato, S Giovanni Battista, S Reparata, SS Apostoli) in Florentine Romanesque style. In the meantime, Florence had won its fight against the local feudal lords and had began battling with neighbouring cities.

The political victory of the bourgeoisie during the 13th century was a result of its economic success. Florentine and Tuscan merchants exported their products to places as far away as London, Bruges and Paris, as well as to the Islamic and Byzantine Orient. In 1252 a gold piece, the florin, was coined – and soon circulated as currency at all the markets of the known world. Up until 1330 Florence remained in the forefront of world trade. Florentines invented numerous elements of today's financial system, including bills of exchange and insurance. Flourishing trade and production drew considerable manpower from the country into the city – following the bourgeois government's abolition of serfdom – while other peasants remained tied to the land around the city through the *mezzadria* system of semi-leasing (whereby landowners split profits with the peasants in return for their labour) which was still being practised right up to the beginning of this century.

Between 1284 and 1333 a third wall was erected around the city which by now contained 100,000 inhabitants. The name Arnolfo di Cambio – the father of Florentine sculpture – is connected with

*Dante Alighieri*

the rebuilding and transformation of S Reparata into the current cathedral. Another impulse of architectural renewal involved the building of the Palazzo dei Priori (today's Signoria). At the same time Cimabue's work sparked a revival in painting culminating in Giotto's achievements. *Volgare*, the spoken language in Florence acquired literary status and, with the help of Dante's *Divina Commedia*, became the national language.

The proliferation of Gothic architecture during the course of the 14th century contributed to the enhancement of Tuscan cities. In Florence, for example, a number of buildings were erected, including Santa Croce, Santa Maria del Fiore and Santa Maria Novella. A throng of painters was needed to cover the walls of these churches with frescoes.

Literature flourished: Boccaccio encouraged the development of a culture based on classical writings as well as on the works of Dante and Petrarch. Italian literature was, at the time, synonymous with Tuscan literature.

In the 14th century, with the plague raging all across Europe bringing medieval civilisation to an end, fighting intensified between the *popolo grasso* (literally: the 'fat people'), ie the big merchants and bankers, and the *popolo minuto* (the 'puny people') consisting of craftsmen and small tradesmen. In Tuscany this period of horror was followed by a radical cultural change: the advancement of Humanism through the Renaissance. In 1434 Cosimo de' Medici began to rule the city as a dictator. He did not, however, assume any public office himself and granted the most powerful families not only substantial tax concessions but also checks and balances on his rule. Those hostile towards his regime, on the other hand, risked being excluded from business activities and thus faced possible financial ruin. Un-

*Detail from Michelangelo's David*

*La Primavera by Sandro Botticelli*

der the patronage of capitalist groups, which had already come to power in 1382, the Renaissance now began to dawn.

Whereas the architectural development of the *trecento* (14th century) had centred around the building of churches, the quattrocento saw a shift of focus to palazzi and aristocratic family chapels – led by Brunelleschi's *palazzo* for Luca Pitti and his chapel for the Pazzi family in Santa Croce. It was at this point that Florence consolidated its fame as a city of artists – Fra Angelico (1400–55), Filippo Lippi (1406–69), Luca della Robbia (1400–82), Andrea del Verrocchio (1435–88), Antonio del Pollaiuolo (1432–98), Domenico Ghirlandaio (1449–94) and Sandro Botticelli (1445–1510), to name only the most important. The best known and most monumental artists, however, were Leonardo da Vinci (1452–1519) and Michelangelo Buonarroti (1475–1564).

Under the rule of the Medici, Neoplatonism became the official state philosophy in Florence, and the Accademia Platonica, founded under Marsilio Ficino, began to convene in Lorenzo de' Medici's villa in Careggi. The Neoplatonists believed in a close connection between philosophical and religious truth, between love and beauty. For a while Lorenzo was able to preserve the political balance in Italy. But the failed attempt of his son and successor, Piero de'Medici, to resist the invading French marked the temporary end of the Medici era. This period was also marked by the steadily growing influence of Girolamo Savonarola, a Dominican monk from Ferrara. Prophesying God's inevitable punishment for Italy's sins, he predicted that from this disaster a new, purified Christianity would emerge. Savonarola was convinced that this radical revival would originate in Florence. An era of austerity began with the official burning of so-called 'vanities'; for example, numerous non-religious paintings by Botticelli were sacrificed to the new ideals. In the end, however, the monk himself was burnt at the stake – which just shows what happens when you get in the way of Florentine business sense and their enjoyment of life.

The appointment to the papacy of two Medici, one shortly after the other, meant an opportunity for their relatives back home, as well as for the monied Florentine bourgeoisie, to make tremendous profits. This practically resulted in a personal union between Rome and Florence. Things went quite well until the year 1527 when the

Empire and the Papacy once again locked horns. Florence resisted the attacking Imperial army. In 1530 the citizens personally took up arms, with Michelangelo supervizing the planning and construction of fortifications. In the end, however, Florence was forced to surrender.

For the first time since the post-Roman barbarian invasions, Florence fell under foreign rule, and – also for the first time since the plague of 1348 – the populace truly suffered. The greatest misfortune, aside from the decline of economic and intellectual activity, was the loss of Republican freedom. This began an era of absolutist rule by Papal appointees of Spanish descent, making Florence a kind of Spanish protectorate. Michelangelo left the city. To prevent Florence from being swallowed totally by the Spanish, the 18-year-old Cosimo I, a distant descendant of the Medici, was made Duke. Putting Machiavellian principles into practice, Cosimo restored limited autonomy, as well as stability to the state. It was only after Cosimo brought neighbouring cities under Florentine rule (through a series

*Savonarola being burnt at the stake in Florence*

of brutal battles) that it was possible to speak of a Tuscan state. Meanwhile, in Rome, Michelangelo became the master to a new generation of artists. Mannerism became the official state art and Giorgio Vasari (1511-74) became not only its most inspired exponent but also the Grand Duchy's 'minister of culture'. This period produced artists such as Bronzino, Benvenuto Cellini, Bartolomeo Ammannati and Bernardo Buontalenti.

Vasari personally undertook changes in Florence's urban development and was responsible for the building of the Uffizi ('offices') – the administration building for the absolutist bureaucracy – along with the Corridoio Vasariano, the connecting passage-way that Vasari built from the Palazzo Vecchio to the seat of the Grand Duke, the Palazzo Pitti.

The 16th century transformed Tuscany, once the cradle of fine art, into a crucible of scientific activity. Galileo Galilei, the father of modern experimental science, was, however, banished. Then the Thirty Years War robbed Tuscany of its markets. This economic crisis was followed by the plague in 1631. The growing decadence of the Medici contributed to political and economic decline.

At the beginning of the 18th century the Tuscans were able to maintain their autonomy by pushing through their demand that the grand ducal Crown remain separate from the imperial one, thus guaranteeing a Tuscan dynasty. In March of 1799 Tuscany was occupied by Napoleon's troops. Defeated by the Austrians and the Russians, the French then withdrew in July of the same year. In 1807, however, Tuscany became part of the French Empire.

The era of the Austrian Dukes of Lorraine, Ferdinand III and Leopold II, saw Tuscany in a sort of hibernation which served to prevent intervention on the part of the Habsburgs, as well as allowing Florence to survive the crises of 1820–1 and 1831 reasonably unharmed. During the four decades following the Restoration much energy was channeled into building and construction. The façade of the Poggio Imperiale, the interior design of the Palazzo Pitti and the buildings in Via Calzaiuoli are examples of the Classicism of this period. The founding of the University of Pisa gave Tuscany a new institution of learning and created a new point of reference for Italy's intelligentsia.

*Santa Croce church*

In 1848 the Tuscan army was massacred in the First War of Independence. On 15 March 1860 the announcement of the annexation of Tuscany by Piedmont provided the decisive jolt for the Union of Italy – which was then proclaimed a year later. For tactical political reasons, Florence was made the capital of Italy from 1865–70 before having to relinquish this status to Rome again.

From this point on, Tuscany and the rest of Italy essentially share the same political history. World War II took a heavy toll in Florence: bridges, entire streets, historic buildings and paintings were destroyed – and in the year 1966 numerous bridges and works of art fell victim to the heavy floods. In 1993, Florence was struck by terrorism but the city rallied and the bomb damage is now virtually repaired.

# Historical Highlights

**700–500BC** Etruscan civilisations, a confederation of states.

**3rd c** The Romans gain power, annexe Etruria and found colonies.

**27** Emperor Augustus assigns the region of Tuscany (up to the Tiber) to Etruria.

**AD467** The fall of Rome.

**493–553** Rule by the Goths.

**553–69** Rule by Byzantium.

**569** Arrival of the Lombards and creation of the Duchy of Tuscia with its seat in Lucca.

**774** After the defeat of the Lombards, the Francs take over Tuscia.

**1000–1300** German emperors conquer Italy. Constant fighting between rival parties, the Guelphs and Ghibellines.

**1118** Consecration of the cathedral in Pisa.

**11th–12th c** Romanesque architecture (exemplified by the Cathedral of Pisa).

**13th–14th c** Gothic architecture: the Cathedral, Santa Maria Novella, Santa Croce and Loggia dei Lanzi in Florence and the Palazzo Pubblico in Siena.

**1348** The plague rages in Florence.

**1384** Arezzo is captured by the Florentines.

**1406** Pisa is defeated and becomes part of the Florentine state.

**1434–64** Cosimo de'Medici, the great art patron, rules Florence.

**1469–92** Lorenzo de'Medici, 'the Magnificent' rules Florence.

**1498** Savonarola is strangled and burned as a heretic.

**1555** Florence defeats and annexes Siena.

**1564–1642** Galileo Galilei: revolutionary discoveries in the field of physics.

**17th–18th c** Baroque period.

**1743** The House of Medici dies out. The Grand Duchy of Tuscany passes to the House of Lorraine.

**1796** Tuscany is occupied by Napoleon's troops.

**1808** Annexation of Tuscany by the French Empire.

**1815** The Grand Duchy is annexed by Austro-Hungarian Monarchy.

**1848** War of Independence.

**1859** Union of Italy.

**1865–70** Florence is the capital city of Italy.

**1870** Rome is made the capital.

**1915** Italy enters the First World War on the side of the Allies.

**1922** Mussolini is made prime minister by Victor Emmanuel.

**1940** Treaty with Germany and Japan; Italy enters the Second World War.

**1943** Overthrow of the Fascists.

**1943–5** Severe war damage; in Florence all the bridges but the Ponte Vecchio are destroyed.

**1945** Execution of Mussolini.

**1946** Italy becomes a republic.

**1957** Treaty of Rome; Italy is a founder member of the EC.

**1966** The Arno floods its banks devastating several sections of Florence and destroying irreplacable works of art and many collections.

**1987** 'Sorpasso' – the Italian economy overtakes that of the British and French.

**1988** Florentines vote for measures to exclude traffic and control pollution.

**1992** Traffic excluded from the Oltrarno area.

**1993** Terrorist bomb damages the Uffizi.

**1995** Regional elections confirm dominance of the Left in Tuscany.

Bologna
Lugo
A14
EMILIA ROMAGNA
Imola
Pavullo
Faenza
Forlì
Porretta Terme
65
12
Castelnuovo
67
Carrara
A12
Massa
65
Pistoia
Forte dei Marmi
A1
Pescia
12
Prato
Viareggio
Montecatini
Terme
Firenze
Lucca
Fièsole
A11
Pontassieve
A11
Bibbiena
Pisa
A12
Arno
Empoli
Impruneta
67
S. Miniato
A1
429
69
S. Gimignano
Arezzo
Livorno
73
Poggibonsi
68
Volterra
Monteriggioni
68
Siena
Corto
Pomarance
TOSCANA
71
Cecina
Mare Mediterraneo
Monte Oliveto
Monticiano
223
Montepulciano
Montalcino
Pienza
Massa
Marittima
Roccastrada
Piombino
223
Cinigiano
Portoferraio
S. Fiora
Elba
Punta Ala
Grosseto
Principina a Mare
Ombrone
Pitigliano
Pianosa
Lago di
Bolseno
Montefiasc
Porto S. Stefano
Orbetello
Giglio
Monte
Argentario
Porto Ercole
635
Montecristo
L
Giannutri

Tuscany, Umbria and The Marches
32 km/ 20 miles
Ravenna
Cervia
Bellaria
Cesena
A 14
71
Rimini
Riccione
Cattolica
S. Marino
SAN MARINO
Pesaro
Fano
sina
Urbino
Fossombrone
Senigallia
73
A 14
Ancona
Mare Adriatico
Ostra
S. Maria di Porto Novo
ansepolcro
Pergola
Iesi
Sirolo
Numana
Osimo
MARCHE
Città di Castello
Cingoli
Recanati
76
Gubbio
Fabriano
Civitanova Marche
Umbertide
Macerata
Tolentino
Perugia
Camerino
Fermo
77
Assisi
Lago Trasimeno
3
A 14
75
Spello
Marsciano
Foligno
Amandola
5
S. Benedetto
Montefalco
Porto d' Ascoli
UMBRIA
Vettore
▲
2478 m
Ascoli Piceno
Todi
Norcia
4
Spoleto
Arquata
vieto
Roseto d. Abruzzi
3
Teramo
Narni
Terni
80
A 14
79
Montereale
Pescara
Penne
Viterbo
Tevere
ABRUZZI
17
ZIO
Rieti
Cittaducale
17
A 1
A 24
L'Aquila
17

# FLORENCE

## TOUR 1



**Cathedral and Baptistry; in Giotto's tower; down Via Calzaiuoli past Orsanmichele, Piazza della Signoria with the Palazzo Vecchio and Loggia dei Lanzi; Ponte Vecchio.**

*Statues, Palazzo Vecchio*

The buildings and places listed above make up the heart of the old city containing the majority of monuments. Here you will also find the best – and unfortunately the most expensive – shops in Florence, as well as restaurants, bars and a great deal more. Nobody lives here any more, especially not since sections of the quarter were made virtually traffic-free zones – the palazzi house almost nothing but offices.

So let us turn our attention to the historic quarter, the *Centro Storico*, as well as to the business section – art and history on the one hand, fashion and pizza *al taglio* (off the baking tray) on the other. These streets offer the *summa* of Florentine art and culture. Our starting point is at the **Piazza del Duomo**. The construction of the Cathedral of Florence – properly called **Santa Maria**

*The Cathedral and Palazzo Vecchio*

**del Fiore** – was actually begun under the supervision of Arnolfo di Cambio during the last years of the 13th century. Brunelleschi, however, was the most important architect: it was he who succeeded in erecting the dome – at that time an almost impossible feat. The present façade was not added until 1888 – construction continued on the cathedral, in other words, for six centuries.

In the mid-16th century Doni wrote that he was convinced that by sitting on the steps outside the cathedral you could hear any language. Standing outside the cathedral today it looks as if that statement remains true. Except on rainy days you will see tourists sitting there from the four corners of the world: eating ice cream, sunning themselves, writing postcards or feeding the pigeons.

The interior of the **Cathedral** (from 9.30am–6pm, admission free) is impressive due to the austerity of its architectural lines – the colours gleam since the recent restoration of the main and south facades. By climbing the 463 steps, you can reach the dome (10am–5pm) and look at the freshly restored Vasari frescoes . The cathedral windows – mostly by Ghiberti, who also created the Paradise Portals of the Baptistry – are remarkable, as are the statues of the prophet Daniel, attributed to Donatello, and the Giotto monument.

Steps lead down to **S. Reparata** in the crypt (open from 10am–5pm), the precursor of the current cathedral going back to the 5th or 6th century. If you are in good shape you should definitely climb to

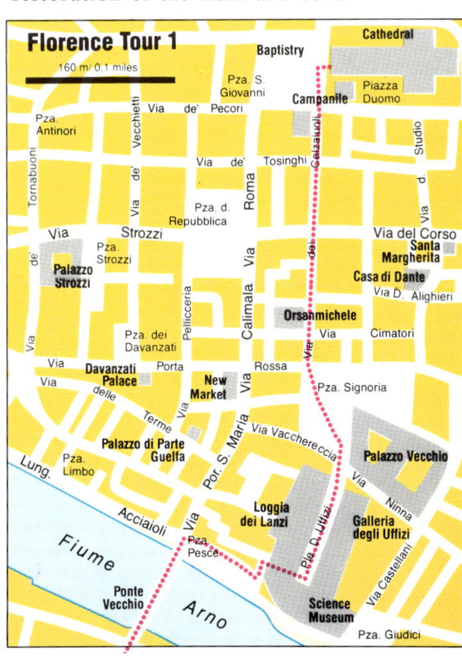

the top of the **Campanile** (from 9am–7.30pm) – the view is ample compensation for tired feet (the restoration of the belltower is due for completion in 1997). Giotto actually intended to build it almost 130ft (40m) higher. Only managing to complete the first storey, however, he had to leave its completion to his successors. On display on the first and second floors you will find ornamentation by Donatello and Pisano – works, for example, such as *The Planets*, *The Virtues* and *The Sacraments*. The steep staircase gets narrower the higher you climb. The window slits along the stairs provide a small glimpse of what awaits you at your destination. The view from the top is like having the most important buildings in Florence presented to you on a tray – making you realize how small the historic heart of Florence really is. See how compact everything is, clustered together, encircled by the usually green Tuscany hills. The red roofs below, fanning out in all directions, are an extraordinary sight which lets you forget the grey tones of concrete that lie beneath some of them. Directly next to us the dome arches upward more mightily than ever.

Back on the ground it is time for a breather: let us spend it in the **Gran Caffè** right next to the Baptistry. Here you can enjoy

*The Cathedral (Duomo)*

the typically Florentine synergy of artistic sensibility and business sense: the bar is heavily patronised because of its frescoes, probably by a Sienese master.

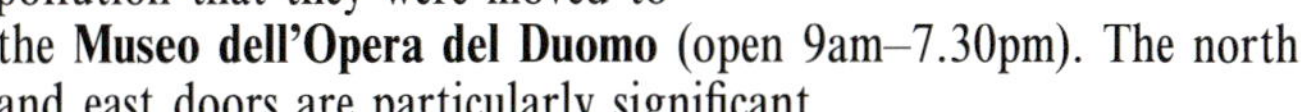

Having refreshed body and soul we are ready to take on the **Paradise Portals** of the Baptistry, three large doors with bronze inlay work, mainly fashioned by Ghiberti. These are, in fact, recently mounted copies – the originals were so damaged by air pollution that they were moved to the **Museo dell'Opera del Duomo** (open 9am–7.30pm). The north and east doors are particularly significant.

The **Baptistry** was erected in the 11th century on the site of a Lombardic or even Early Christian building (which is why it was long assumed to be a Roman temple). Up until the 19th century the Baptistry was the only baptismal chapel in Florence. An unusual method was used to count those awaiting baptism: beans were placed for each child in a bowl by the door – a dark bean meant a little boy, a light one a little girl. Dante, amongst others, was baptized here. Inside you will find frescoes of *The Last Judgement*, the work of a 13th century Venetian master on which the young Giotto may have collaborated.

In the **Loggia del Bigallo**, or rather in the museum in this building – at the corner of **Via Calzaiuoli** (Cobbler's Alley) – you will find a fresco dated 1342 showing the oldest surviving view of Florence. Via Calzaiuoli is one of the main shopping streets – and the prices are accordingly high. How about trying an ice cream on Via de' Tavolini, the second street on the left? **Perché no?** ('Why not?') is one of the best ice cream parlours in Florence. Personally, I prefer to have a glass of red wine at the vineria on **Via dei Cimatori**. There used to be plenty of these little wine bars where you could just have a sip of wine in passing – for the Tuscans like to see to it that their blood alcohol level does not drop too low. Note also the shop next door where advertising signs are made.

Across the street is the **Orsanmichele** church – the name being a contraction of *Orti* (gardens) *di San Michele*. This strange building used to double as a granary and an oratory. The lower floor was an open-columned hall where hawkers could seek shelter from the sun and rain. In Florence commerce and prayer have always been inseparable. Later the building also became the seat of the guilds. The statues in the exterior niches are predominantly by Ghiberti. To the right you will find the **Palazzo dell'Arte della Lana** or 'wool guild palace' consisting of three buildings dating from the 13th century and connected with Orsanmichele by Vasari's 'covered

*Palazzo Vecchio detail*

catwalk'. The ground floor is occupied by Zanobetti, one of the most tasteful clothing stores in Florence. If you like, you can make a small detour to the beautiful **Palazzo di Parte Guelfa**, once the seat of the Guelf Party.

The next stop is the **Mercato Nuovo**, the airy loggia housing the old straw market. Everything except straw goods are for sale, from flowers to embroidered tablecloths. The buyers are mostly tourists, naturally – who can improve their chances of returning to Florence by patting the nose of the bronze boar *Porcellino* ('piglet') sitting out front.

Then we follow **Via Vacchereccia** to **Piazza della Signoria**. Outside the **Palazzo Vecchio** there are several statues – the best-known being the omnipresent *David* (a copy; the original is in the Museum of the Accademia, 60 Via Ricasoli). Donatello's *Judith* (also a copy) stands next to him. The original is inside, in the Sala delle Udienze. *Judith* and *David* are embodiments of the Republican idea of freedom, for Judith liberated her people from the tyranny of Holofernes and David rescued his land from the threat of the giant, Goliath.

The *Neptune* fountain, which the Florentines call *Biancone* ('White Giant'), was installed in honour of the wedding of Francesco de'Medici and Joanna of Austria. Just before you reach it, look for a sign on the ground marking the spot where the Dominican monk Savonarola was burnt at the stake.

The inner courtyard of the Palazzo Vecchio is noteworthy for its painted views of the free cities of the old German Empire – an additional homage to the Habsburg bride; the rooms inside, such as the Salone dei Cinquecento (the council chamber) and, on the second floor, the Quartieri Monumentali (state apartments) offer additional attractions (open from 9am–7pm; Sunday and Friday from 8am–1pm, closed on Saturday; there is also an entrance for the handi-

*The Uffizi across the Arno*

capped). The municipal offices are located at the back of the Palazzo Vecchio, which is why you may well meet a wedding party or two around here.

*Piazza della Signoria*

Back outside you have the **Uffizi** where you may want to spend the rest of the afternoon, and where you can make your way to the terrace café located on top of the **Loggia dei Lanzi** (reached through the west corridor of the gallery).

On returning to the Piazza della Signoria, you can inspect the Loggia from ground level. Opened in 1381, this Loggia was once the meeting place of the municipal government. The most important statues sheltering here are Cellini's *Perseus* and the *Rape of the Sabine Women* by Giambologna. By now you have deserved a treat. Sitting in the sun drinking a cup of coffee outside chic café **Rivoire** is pure enjoyment.

If you still feel like walking, go down **Por Santa Maria** to the **Ponte Vecchio**, the oldest bridge in Florence. As early as the 13th century craftsmen had set up shop on the bridge. Only jewellers and goldsmiths were allowed to do business here because anything else would have been too 'dirty' in the eyes of the Grand Duke Ferdinand I. **Corridoio Vasariano**, the overhead passage connecting the Palazzo Vecchio and the Palazzo Pitti, crosses this bridge. If you don't want to shop for elegant jewellery, just enjoy the views from the bridge and the stream of passers-by.

## The Silver Arno

**Piazza Santa Maria Novella with its churches; along the Arno; Via de' Tornabuoni, Florence's most elegant street; Palazzo Strozzi.**

Only recently has **Piazza S. Maria Novella** become fully enjoyable: before they blocked off the traffic to non-residents it was the scene of traffic jams with the usual honking and suffocating fumes. Today you can sit on a bench and take in the serenity and regularity of the church façade designed by Leon Battista Alberti – largely forgetting the modern world of the train station behind it.

The Dominican church of **Santa Maria Novella** was completed in 1300 with financial support from the Florentine merchant Giovanni Rucellai. Not surprisingly, in this city saturated with history, this building, too, had a predecessor: the church of Santa Maria della Vigna (Holy Mary of the Vineyard) was surrounded by vineyards and went back to the year 1064. Inside, the frescoes by Ghirlandaio with his self-portrait are a must, as well as works by Masaccio (*The Trinity*) and Giotto (a crucifix) (open Monday to Saturday from 7–11:30am and 3:30–6pm).

To the right of the church is the **Museo di Santa Maria Novella**, incorporating the Chiostro Verde with works by Paolo Uccello (open weekdays from 9am–2 pm, weekends from 8am–1 pm, closed Friday). The church also offers interesting frescoes in the **Cappellone degli Spagnoli**, the former chapter hall, which in 1556 was placed at the disposal of the Spanish community in Florence. One of the frescoes depicts some black and white dogs – an allegorical reference to the Dominicans (*domini canes*), the 'Dogs of Our Lord'.

Purified and strengthened we head to the right off Piazza Santa Maria Novella into **Via della Scala**. Even if you do not intend to buy anything (I highly recommend the soaps and creams, as well

*Santa Maria Novella*

as the Dominican-brewed liqueur), you should definitely peek inside the old pharmacy at No. 16. Otherwise, pop across the street to the **Caffè Voltaire**; in the evenings jazz concerts and other performances are often held here.

After this refreshing stop we continue down Via della Scala and **Via della Vigna Nuova** with their elegant shops and splendid palazzi (the Palazzo Rucellai houses the Alinari photography museum) to the **Ponte alla Carraia**, the second oldest bridge in the city. It has been standing since 1218; the current version, however, goes back to 1559. From here you can see the **Ponte Santa Trinita**, the oldest bridge (erected in 1257, washed away and rebuilt, destroyed by the Germans in 1945 and reconstructed in 1957) and of course the **Ponte Vecchio**. Unfortunately it is a long time since the waters of the Arno were silver – as described in the famous song, *Arno d'argento* – and a bit more greenery along the paved shores would also be nice – but no, we might as well accept the fact: Florence *is* a city of stone – with even its gardens hidden and accessible only from within the buildings.

Our route now takes us across the bridge and along **Lungarno Guicciardini** (note the magnificent palazzi on the right and left banks of the Arno, especially the Palazzo

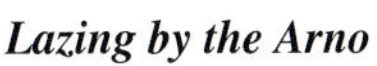

*Lazing by the Arno*

*Ponte Vecchio*

Corsini on the opposite bank with its famous private collection) to the **Ponte Santa Trinita** (if you are particularly in a hurry, you can stay on the same side of the river and walk along Lungarno Corsini). From here, cross the bridge into **Via de'Tornabuoni**, the most elegant shopping street in Florence. The corner, at **Lungarno Acciaiuoli**, is dominated by the mighty **Palazzo Spini Ferroni**, one of the largest medieval palazzi, whose construction was begun in 1289. Today it is the headquarters of the famous shoe company Ferragamo – Florence was and will remain the city of merchants.

On **Piazza Santa Trinita** there is the church of the same name going back to the 14th century (the previous building on the same site existed as early as 1077); the façade was finished in 1593. The interior (open 7am–noon and 4–7pm) still bears characteristic Gothic elements. Like so many churches it contains chapels commissioned and decorated by wealthy merchant families hoping to ensure their souls' salvation – the most important being the **Cappella Sassetti** with its Ghirlandaio frescoes. The main wall bears a representation of Piazza della Signoria with the Palazzo Vecchio and the Loggia dei Lanzi, while on the right we see the donor, Francesco Sassetti, between his son and his friend Lorenzo de' Medici. This is the most important contemporary portrait of Lorenzo.

The fresco *Miracle of the Resurrected Boy* portrays Santa Trinita with its former Romanesque façade and Palazzo Spini Ferroni where the boy had fallen out of a window.

A *panino tartufato*, truffle sandwich at **Procacci** (64r Via Tornabuoni, on the right side of the street) accompanied by a glass of red wine – that is always a pleasure which we would not like to do without in this somewhat dusty city. If, however, this has only whetted your appetite and you are still feeling hungry, then I recommend you walk further down **Via de' Tornabuoni** to the **Cantinetta Antinori** (3 Piazza Antinori). My personal tip: *crostini all toscana* and *pappa al pomodoro* with a glass of *Sassicaia or Antinori brut*. It will not be cheap, but it is worth it to appreciate the panelled interior and the wines and cheeses from the family estate.

The **Palazzo Antinori** is one of the few buildings in Florence continuously owned by one and the same family – since 1506. **San Gaetano**, the baroque-like church across the street was mentioned as early as the 11th century.

*Piazza della Repubblica*

We now return to **Via del Strozzi** and to the **Palazzo Strozzi**. Its size, (like that of the Palazzo Rucellai) demonstrates how keen the owner was on erecting a monument to himself. Filippo Strozzi had astrologers calculate precisely the most favourable time during the year 1489 for the laying of the foundation stone. To build this 'detached family house' so that two façades would be visible simultaneously from a number of different perspectives, Filippo Strozzi had 15 buildings torn down to create this overweening monstrosity, currently closed for major restoration work.

So we have seen what a Florentine house looks like from the outside, but what is it like to live in one? The forerunner of all palazzi, the **Palazzo Davanzati** houses the **Museo della Casa Fiorentina Antica** with its well-furnished rooms dating from the 14th century, complete with charming courtyard and a medieval kitchen (Piazza Davanzati; open from 9am–2pm; Sundays 9am–noon; closed Monday; holidays from 9am–1pm).

Had enough of Renaissance, of churches and museums for today? Why not treat yourself to an aperitif at **Gilli**'s on **Piazza della Repubblica** (note the Belle Epoque interior decoration), the playground for all those who wish to be seen. *Salute!*

## Gothic Florence

**The Badia; Bargello; Santa Croce; the flea market; and a typical Tuscan restaurant.**

The area around **Badia** (Via del Proconsolo) and **Bargello** (Via del Proconsolo/corner of Via Ghibellina) makes up the centre of medieval Florence. The **Badia** (abbey) was the church of the wealthiest monastery in the medieval city – founded by Benedictines in the 10th century. The first pre-Romanesque building is no longer standing and all that remains of the second building begun in 1285 is a portion of the apse. In 1627 the church was restructured to give it a baroque appearance. Inside you will discover Filippo Lippi's Holy Virgin appearing before St Bernard and the Chiostro degli Aranci, a chrming loggia where the monks grow oranges.

The **Bargello** (Old Italian for 'the thug'), the oldest palazzo surviving from the communal period (1254–61) was both a fortified prison and the seat of the mayor. Today the massive building with the beautiful courtyard – where from 1502–1782 death sentences were carried out – houses the National Museum with the most significant works of Florentine sculpture (works by Michelangelo, Giambologna, Donatello, Verrocchio; open daily from 9am–2pm, Sunday 9am to 1pm, closed Monday).

Heading along the **Via dell'Anguillara**, one of the oldest streets

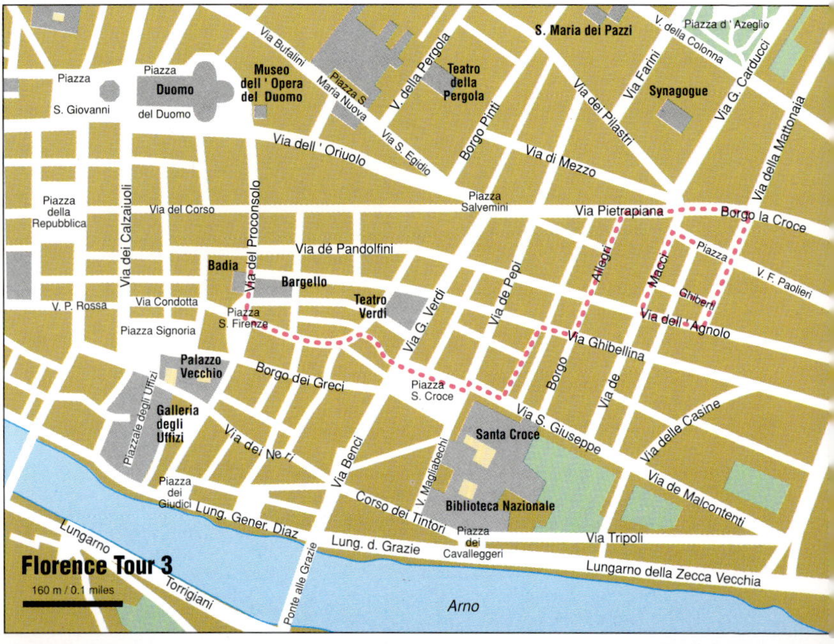

**Florence Tour 3**

160 m / 0.1 miles

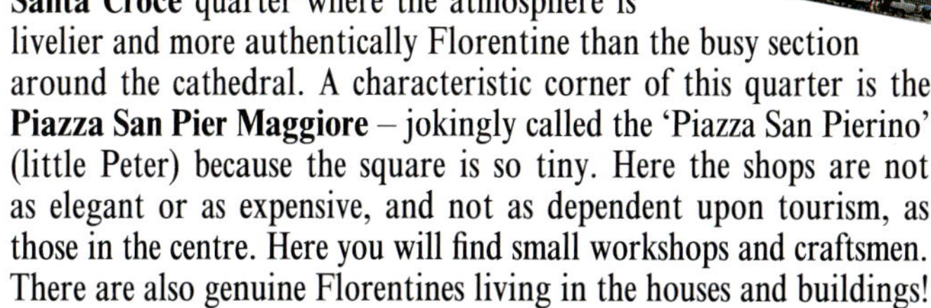

in the city, where Michelangelo had his first workshop, we reach the **Piazza S Simone**. A legend around the world, **Bar Vivoli** is *the* ice-cream parlour. The area is criss-crossed with narrow alleys: the **Via Torta** ('crooked alley') is quite unusual – its name derives from the fact that it was built around the curving wall of a former Roman amphitheatre.

We are now standing in the **Santa Croce** quarter where the atmosphere is livelier and more authentically Florentine than the busy section around the cathedral. A characteristic corner of this quarter is the **Piazza San Pier Maggiore** – jokingly called the 'Piazza San Pierino' (little Peter) because the square is so tiny. Here the shops are not as elegant or as expensive, and not as dependent upon tourism, as those in the centre. Here you will find small workshops and craftsmen. There are also genuine Florentines living in the houses and buildings!

The large, square **Piazza Santa Croce** – the site of the annual historical *Calcio in Costume*, a football game played in Renaissance clothing – is surrounded by 15th and 16th century palazzi (pay special attention to the Palazzo Cocchi Serristori and, opposite it, the Palazzo dell'Antella, south side, Nos 21–22). The Gothic **Santa Croce Church** (what a difference from Northern European Gothic!) was erected by Franciscans – as far away as possible from their rivals, the Dominicans of San Marco – in 1226, shortly after the death of St Francis of Assisi (church open from 8am–6:30pm; adjoining museum open 10am–12.30 and 2.30–6.30pm). The building was completed in 1380; the facade, like that of the Cathedral, dates from the 19th century.

The recently restored interior is dominated by Florentine austerity and Franciscan simplicity combined with the large spaciousness of Early Christian basilicas; the chapels of the Bardi and Peruzzi families – a family chapel in Santa Croce was *the* status symbol in Trecento Florence – has frescoes by Giotto and members of his workshop. Another privilege enjoyed by very few was to be buried here, in the Florentine Pantheon, including Michelangelo, Galileo and Machiavelli. The empty sarcophagus next to Michelangelo's gravestone is noteworthy: this is where Dante, first banished from Florence and then asked to return, was meant to lie. But the city of Ravenna, where the poet died, never returned his remains.

You have to leave the church in order to look around the **Pazzi Chapel**, the former chapter house. Attributed to Brunelleschi, this Early Renaissance building (1430) creates an impressive contrast to the Gothic church; in the adjoining **Museo dell'Opera di Santa Croce** a crucifix by Cimabue is eye-catching.

The **Via delle Pinzochere** will take you to **Casa Buonarroti** (Via

Ghibellina 70) which once belonged to Michelangelo, though he never lived here. The museum in the house has two of Michelangelo's early works. Following **Borgo Allegri**, the street in Florence with the worst reputation, we arrive at the **Piazza dei Ciompi**, where you can rummage around at the flea market.

Heading to the right into the **Via Pietrapiana** and across the **Piazza S Ambrogio** (with a 15th–16th-century church) will take you to the food market on the **Piazza Ghiberti**. Cibreo (Via de' Macci 118r) is a touchstone of Tuscan cusine, the place for an aperitif or a snack, lunch or dinner.

**The Palazzo Pitti Museum in the morning; after relaxing in the Boboli Gardens a walk through the characteristic San Frediano quarter with its Santo Spirito, Carmine and Cestello churches.**

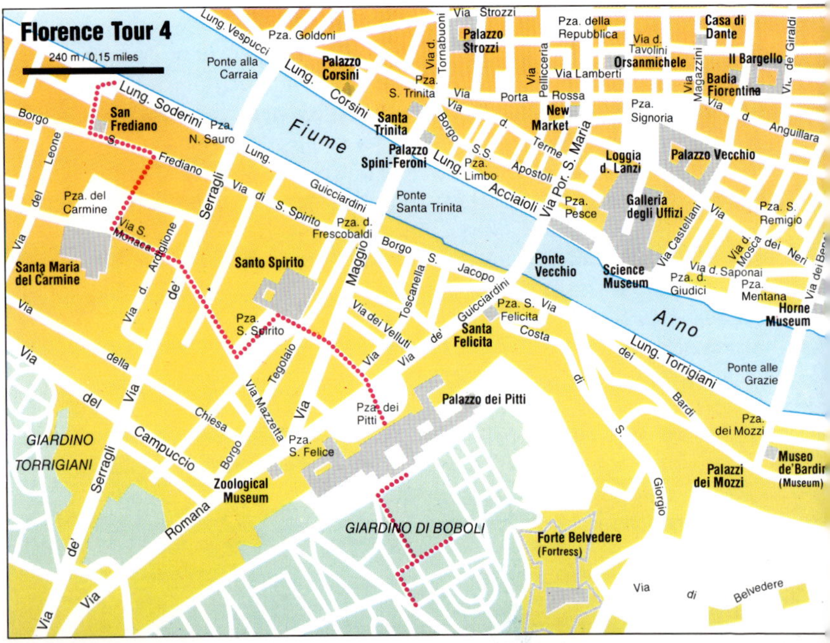

To get off to a good start, we will have breakfast in the **Caffè** at 9 Piazza de' Pitti before embarking on an exploration of the Oltrarno, the once modest south bank of the Arno that rose to prominence under the Medici. **Palazzo Pitti** was built for the wealthy merchant Luca Pitti in 1457 and in 1549 was bought and

extended by Eleonora of Toledo, the wife of Cosimo I. The building then remained the royal seat of the Medici and the Grand Dukes of Tuscany for three centuries. In fact, from the heyday of the Medici until modern times, the palace was lived in by the city rulers. During the time of Napoleon, Bonaparte's sister, the Queen of Etruria, lived here. Until 1949 the Palazzo was the residence of members of the House of Savoy.

Although it has not been clearly determined who the architect of this huge building was, Brunelleschi may have provided the blueprints. Inside we find the **Galleria Palatina** containing the private collection of the Grand Dukes of Tuscany (opening times for all the museums in the Palazzo Pitti: 9am–2pm; holidays 9am–1pm; closed Monday). The works displayed range from Renaissance to Baroque with highlights by Raphael and Titian, as well as by Rubens and Van Dyck. The **Galleria d'Arte Moderna** offers mainly 19th-century paintings: works by the Tuscan *Macchiaioli*, late 19th-century Impressionists whose number included Giovanni Fattori, Telemaco Signorini and Giovanni Boldini. The **Museo degli Argenti** boasts worked gold and silver, while the Appartamenti Monumentali are the splendidly restored state apartments.

If we are in luck and the sun is shining, I would recommend a walk around the **Boboli Gardens**, a prime example of gardening *all'italiana*. The prettiest part is Isolotto (Little Island), the southern portion nearest the Porta Romana. The gardens are decorated with hundreds of marble statues – one of the best-known being the Fontano di Bacco, the Bacchus Fountain, set close to the Pitti

*Santo Spirito*

Palace. The rider on the turtle was actually the court dwarf of Cosimo I.

Other features of the garden include the rococo building that even the Italians call by the German name **Kaffeehaus**, since it was built for the Austrian nobleman, Peter Leopold of Habsburg-Lorraine. Then there is the neoclassical building, La Meridiana, that contains the **Galleria del Costume** with its gowns and costumes of eras gone by. The Grand Dukes raised silkworms in the Giardino del Cavaliere and this is where the first potato from America was planted in Italy.

Back outside we cross the Piazza de' Pitti and continue straight ahead into the alley called **Scrucciolo de' Pitti** leading to **Via Maggio**. Once intended as the triumphant approach to Mannerist Florence, today Via Maggio is the antique dealers' street. At No 26 Via Maggio we discover the house built by Buontalenti from 1570–74 for Bianca Cappello – first the mistress, then the wife of Ferdinando de'Medici; it is a fine example of the decorated palazzi of the end of the Cinquecento.

We now arrive in the **San Frediano** quarter where you will encounter few tourists, even in the high season, and where the traditional Florentine lifestyle still thrives. This is evident in the numerous workshops and the crowds of people in the street – the atmosphere being one of bustling activity, not of stress and strain. Next we reach the **Piazza Santo Spirito** with, on your right, the church of the same name (open 8am–noon and 4–6pm), built by Brunelleschi from 1434–82, with its elegant, unfinished façade.

The Augustinians who had the first building erected here in the 13th century also provided quarters for itinerants, a hospital for the sick and a kitchen for the needy. Later their monastery became a centre of humanistic education: Boccaccio left them his library.

Legend has it that for years the monks did without one meal a day to finance the elaborate new building created by Brunelleschi. As with so many of his projects, Brunelleschi did not live to see this building completed. Unfortunately the intended overall effect is disturbed by elements added later, such as the baroque baldacchino over the altar. Better by far, in the **Cenacolo di Santo Spirito**, the refectory and museum adjoining Santo Spirito, is a *Crucifixion* fresco from the original monastery. The square outside (note the *palazzo* on the corner of Via Mazzetta, built in 1503 for the wealthy silk merchant Rinieri Dei) was the meeting place for the 'in' crowd in the Seventies with the **Bar Ricchi** as its focal point (perhaps you would like to take a seat in the sun for a glass of *prosecco*). Since the 1980s, however, the local scene has converged on the nearby **Plazza del Carmine** (follow Via S Agostino and Via Santa Monaca to get there). But the atmosphere is totally different: **Dolce Vita** is the youthful haunt of today's hedonists.

Here, too, you will find an important church: **Santa Maria del**

*In the Boboli Gardens*

**Carmine** (open 7am–noon and 3.30–7pm). Begun for the Carmelite Order in 1268, the original Florentine Gothic building was destroyed by a fire in 1771. Fortunately the famous **Brancacci Chapel** (only 15-minute visits allowed) with its revolutionary Masaccio frescoes were saved. Having begun the chapel's frescoes around 1424, Masolino left Florence while Masaccio took over until his return – after which the two painters completed significant portions together. After both died Filippino Lippi completed the cycle in 1485. It is not easy to distinguish the work of the three different painters – Masolino still used the soft lines of international Gothic, whereas Masaccio is much more dramatic and expressive.

Crossing **Borgo San Frediano** we approach a true gem, the small baroque church of **San Frediano in Cestello** whose dome, overlooking the river Arno, is a local landmark. If you have delevoped an appetite stop in at **Angiolino** (36, Via Santo Spirito); for a snack try **Cantinone del Gallo Nero** (6r, Via Santo Spirito) where you can also quench your thirst, particularly for wine.

## Tracking Down the Medici

**Renaissance culture and then lively market chaos: the clothing market and the food market; followed by lunch.**

Piazza SS Annunziata ('SS' stands for *Santissima* – exceptionally holy) is near the university (Piazza Brunelleschi). Coming from the west it actually marks the beginning of the city centre. The *loggia* (arcade) of the **Spedale degli Innocenti**, built by Brunelleschi around 1420 and containing *tondi* (roundels) by Luca della Robbia, was copied on the opposite side a century later by Antonio da Sangallo. The unity which this gave to the piazza was so pleasing that the loggia was extended in front of the church, creating an ensemble which emanates a strong sense of calm. Looking across the street you will see the **Palazzo Budini Gattai** on the right, today the seat of the Tuscan state government, and on the left the hotel, Loggiato de Serviti, with its antique furnishings. The statue of **Ferdinando de'Medici** which dominates the square is modelled on the statue of Marcus Aurelius in the Campidoglio in Rome.

The portico of **SS Annunziata**, also known as the *Chiostrino dei Vati*, contains frescoes by Andrea del Sarto, who also created the *Madonna del Sacco* and the *Madonna de Morti* inside. Numerous 16th-century artists

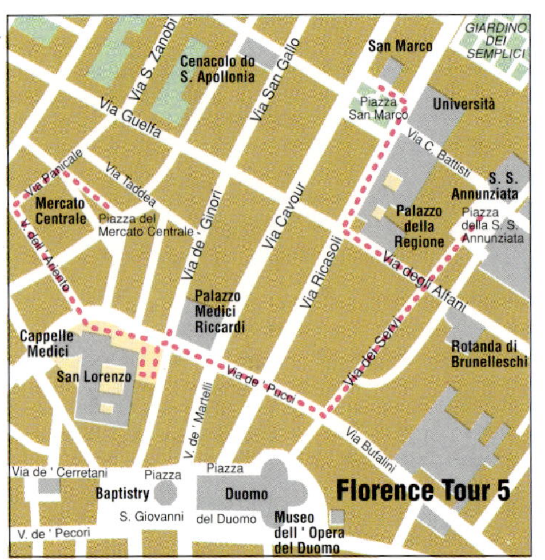

*San Lorenzo*

(eg Leon Battista Alberti) are buried within this church.

In the **Galleria dello Spedale** degli Innocenti the *Madonna e Angelo* by Botticelli and the *Epifania* by Ghirlandaio (open daily 9am–2pm, Sunday 9am–1pm, closed Wednesday) are especially worth mentioning. A large portion of the Medici collection of ancient art is housed nearby in the **Museo Archeologico**, including the Etruscan Statues *Chimera*, *Idolino* and *The Actor* (36 Via della Colonna; open Tuesday to Saturday 9am–2pm; Sunday 9am–1pm).

The next stop is practically a must: **San Marco** monastery, on the piazza of the same name, is reached by heading left down Via Battisti (open 9am–2pm, closeed Monday). Taking in the gentle frescoes by Fra Angelico in the modest cells where the austere monk, Savonarola, once lived, you may wind up asking yourself why our way of living requires so many material things. In Florence, fortunately, all the interesting sights are close together, so while you are searching for that answer you can wander the short walk down to the **Accademia** (careful: the emphasis is on the 'e') in **Via Ricasoli** (open 9am–7pm, Sunday 9am–1pm, closed Monday). Here the real *David* self-confidently 'holds his own', but hardly manages to steal the show from the unfinished *Prigioni* (also by Michelangelo). A few years ago a well-known company gave a PR banquet at the foot of *David*; postcards and T-shirts offer further examples of the abuse which poor David has to put up with.

How about a breather – a glass of wine perhaps at **Fani**'s on the corner of **Via degli Alfani** and **Via de Servi**? Or, if you prefer, a *cappuccino* on **Piazza San Marco** at the bar of the same name. Then continue down **Via Cavour** to **Fetrinelli** bookstore, meeting place of Florentine students and intellectuals (they also have a good stock of foreign-language books). Looking across the street you will see the **Palazzo Medici Riccardi**. Originally intended as the town residence of the Medici, the building also housed the administrative offices of the family bank as well as the commercial headquarters. If you want to take a look inside, the **Cappella del Palazzo** is worth your time for the newly restored frescoes by

*San Lorenzo market*

Benozzo Gozzoli, painted in the style of the Flemish Masters from 1452 to 1460. The frescoes include portraits of several members of the Medici family. The frescoes in the **Luca Giordano Room**, on the other hand, are a veritable apotheosis of the Medici (open 9am–1pm, Sundays and holidays 3–6pm, closed Wednesday).

Returning to the street, turn immediately right into Via de' Gori. Practically hidden behind the sales carts, the *barroccini*, you will find **S Lorenzo Church** – the first truly Renaissance church. It was built by Filippo Brunelleschi from 1421–69, although its origin goes back to Early Christian times (it is one of the oldest churches in Florence).

In 1418 when construction work began to expand the church, an entire neighbourhood was torn down to make room. Soon, however, work had to be halted, since the long-running war against the neighbouring town of Lucca had drained the city treasury. Thus it was that Cosimo de'Medici offered to finance the remaining work. This is how S Lorenzo became the family church of the Medici. Only the façade remains unfinished – since nobody could agree on the design. Today Florentines say that the façade is more beautiful as it is, besides fitting the rustic Palazzo Medici better this way. Inside are works by Donatello and Filippo Lippi.

Next to the church (to your left when you are facing the main portal) there is also a **library** bearing the name 'Medici' – having been erected on behalf of Pope Clement VII (one of Lorenzo's brothers; open Monday to Saturday 9am–1pm; admission is free). This room by Michelangelo represents a prime example of the Mannerist style in Renaissance architecture. In 1990 there were veritable street battles outside the church between the *ambulanti*, the owners of the street carts, and the police who attempted to enforce an ordinance passed by the city administration banishing street traders. Quite in keeping with the Biblical example, the police sought to banish the merchants from the steps of the church. The police failed, and it is not just tourists who shop here, at the **mercantino**: Florentines do so as well since the prices are quite low. Bargaining, however, is no longer the usual thing – at the most you might be able to bargain the price down 5,000 lire. You will find all types of clothing on display here, as well as leather goods, table-cloths, shoes and plenty of other things.

We now proceed through the market and around the church (there are good views of beautiful roof gardens on the various palazzi) until we reach **Piazza della Madonna degli Aldobrandini** on our left. There we find the **Cappelle Medicee** (9am–2pm, closed Monday), conceived as a magnificent mausoleum. The atmosphere inside the marble **Cappella dei Principi** is oppressive and gloomy, a rare example of Baroque architectural style in Florence. What a contrast: the

**Sagrestia Nuova** (1524) contains the famous sculptures by Michelangelo (Lorenzo, the brooder, between *Dawn* (feminine) and *Dusk* (masculine); Giuliano, the man of action, between *Day* and *Night*). Malicious Florentines say that the female figures look rather unfeminine, claiming that Michelangelo (being homosexual) never set eyes on a naked woman in his entire life. Art historians, on the other hand, assume that he simply preferred male models.

The **Sagrestia Vecchia** (Brunelleschi) and **Sagrestia Nuova** (Michelangelo) mark the beginning and end of the Renaissance: it is astonishing that these two significant works are located in one and the same building, making it possible to view them back-to-back.

By now, it is high time we looked after our physical well-being: on the right, in **Via dell'Ariento** you have the **Casa del Vino** (wine and snack bar) with a guaranteed local Florentine clientele. The more courageous souls among you may try a *panino con la trippa or panino col lampredotto* (tripe or pig's intestine sandwiches) at the cart across from the Pasticceria Sieni. If you have a larger appetite, you can walk across the street to the **Mercato Centrale**, the market hall where you can not only buy meat, fish, vegetables and fruit, but also enjoy Tuscan cooking – with a crash course in authentic Tuscan cursing thrown in.

Behind the market, in **Via Rosina**, there is more genuine Florentine atmosphere in concentrated form waiting for you. Despite the considerable crowd of hungry guests, you hardly ever have to wait long for a seat; equally you will hardly have swallowed your last bite when you will be 'asked' to leave – with typical Florentine friendliness ('You're still stuffing your face?!'). But the place is cheap and the food is good! Should you desire something more noble, however, you will be better off at the restaurant **Taverna del Bronzino** (Via delle Ruote, approximately 10-minute walk), which is more stylish and more expensive.

## Romans and Etruscans

**Today we head five miles (8km) to the northwest of Florence, to the delightful town of Fiesole, a popular escape located on top of a hill.**

Fiesole was first settled by Etruscans in the 7th century BC. The Romans who followed named the place *Faesulum* – praising it for its river bed and its ideal location for controlling the entire valley. Despite this, the town was repeatedly attacked by the Goths and Byzantines. In 1125 the city was destroyed by Florentine troops – only the cathedral and the bishop's palace were saved. Thus the city lost both its autonomy and its economic and political power. During the 15th century Fiesole was a suburb where wealthy Florentines built their villas – and this fact has remained unchanged to this day. A villa in Fiesole, on the slopes of the hill, is one of *the* exclusive addresses. At the same time the town has managed to preserve a village-like character – especially above Piazza Mino.

Today **Fiesole** is the place to go for an outing – escaping from the oppressive heat on hot summer evenings or from the hurly-burly of the city. You have the choice of either taking a taxi (note: the drivers charge extra because Fiesole lies outside the Florence city limits) or taking Bus No 7 from Piazza Stazione or from Piazza San Marco, which takes about 35 minutes. Another alternative (for the very energetic) is to rent a bicycle. The views from the car or bus on the way up reveal a landscape of extraordinary beauty, dotted with numerous Renaissance villas perched on the slope of the hill.

Arriving at **Piazza Mino da Fiesole** the first thing you will notice is the **Duomo di San Romolo**, begun in 1028 and thoroughly renovated in 1878. Some of the cahtedral's capitals are Roman. Across the way you can see the episcopal palace, which dates back to the 11th century, with a façade that was finished in 1675. Further up the square, the **Palazzo Pretorio**, with its coats of arms and emblems, dates back to the 14th century; the equestrian statue in front of it

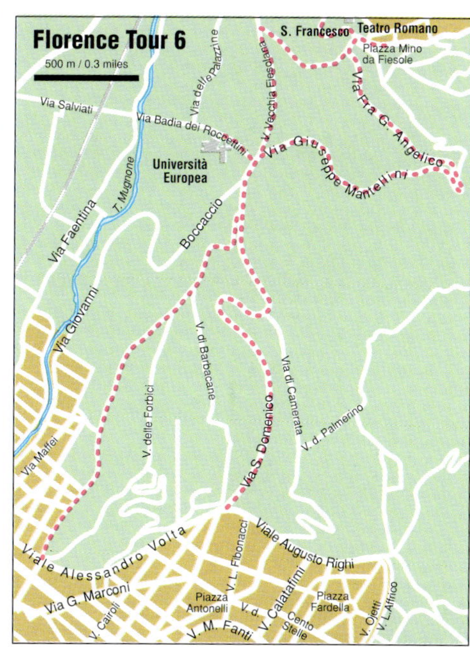

*Roman amphitheatre in Fiesole*

commemorates the encounter between Vittorio Emanuele II and Garibaldi.

Next to the Palazzo Pretorio you will find the small church of **Santa Maria Primerana**, originally medieval but rebuilt in the 16th century. Inside you will discover frescoes and a 14th-century crucifix. The church was designed for ordinary people to use on an everyday basis, whereas the cathedral was used for ceremonies and special celebrations.

Following **Via Portigiani** will take you to the well-preserved **Roman amphitheatre** built in the 1st century BC and capable of holding up to 3,000 spectators (open 9am–7pm, in the winter from 10am–4pm; closed on holidays). The thermal baths to the right of the theatre are still equipped with a large tub, the remnants of the heating installations and components of the facilities, such as the *calidarium, sudarium, tepidarium* and the *frigidarium*. There are two altars in front of the Roman temple: the larger being Roman, the smaller Etruscan.

The theatre is the venue of the *Estate Fiesolana,* a cultural festival held from June through August. Attending a performance is highly rec-

*Roman ruins in Fiesole*

ommended, if only for the lovely setting (it gets chilly, however, so a sweater is a must!).

The adjoining **Museo Civico** presents a selection of Roman and Etruscan material recovered from excavations. The **Museo Bandini** in Via Duprè 1 features Trecanto paintings along with sculpture, majolica and furniture (open 10am–1pm and 3–6pm, closed Tuesday). If you are not particularly interested in history or art, I suggest you skip these two museums and spend the time enjoying the surrounding *campagna*, which is glorious.

*San Francesco*

An absolute must, on the other hand, is the walk up to **San Francesco**. The narrow, steep road (Via di San Francesco; to the right the restaurant **La Loggia degli Etruschi** has a pretty view) begins across from the façade of the cathedral and features two lookout points (the first toward the east, the second toward the south). The view of the valley with Florence and the Arno winding its way among the hills is unique.

The boring neoclassical façade of the church of **Sant' Alessandro** hides a more exciting interior: a 9th-century basilica with Ionic capitals and columns of Greek marble and a timber ceiling (open daily from 7–12am, 3–6.30pm). Further up the hill, **San Francesco** was first a home for gentlewomen before becoming a Franciscan monastery in 1399. At the beginning of this century the buildings were over-restored, but the overall impression of the church, cloister and monastic cells is quite convincing. The museum run by the Franciscan Order displays missionaries' souvenirs from all over the world.

Now it is time to head back down to the piazza for a well-deserved breather: the square has no shortage of bars and cafés, most with fine views over the olive-clad hills. We will take another route on the way back to Florence: the hikers among us should go on foot; the less athletic can ask a taxi driver to follow this route which the bus does not take. Following **Via Vecchia Fiesolana**, we arrive at **S Domenico**. This charming 15th-century church features frescoes by Fra Angelico, who lived here before he transferred to San Marco in Florence. A detour to the right, down **Via dei Roccettini**, will take you to **Badia Fiesolana**, the lovely former cathedral of Fiesole, now swallowed up by the European university complex. The Badia, with its geometric Romanesque facade, is only open on Sunday morning.

Back at S Domenico you can either take Bus No 7 or – if you still have the stamina – walk back along **Via della Piazzola**, a narrow lane lined with old villas. From Piazza delle Cure, Bus No 1 will take you back into the centre of town.

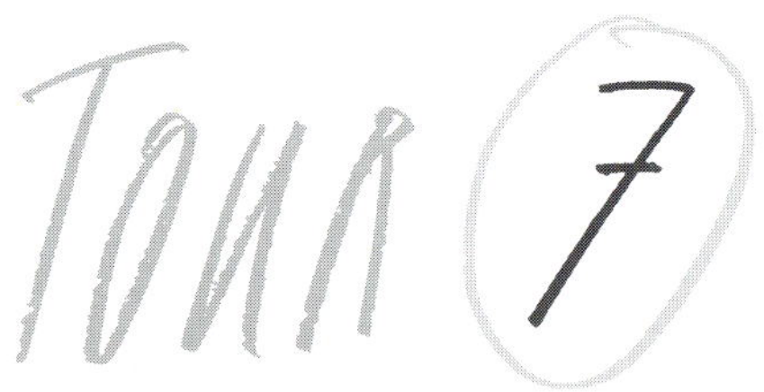




**Great views: Viali de Colli; to Piazzale Michelangelo; returning via Via San Leonardo with Forte Belvedere; to San Niccolo'.**

For this walking tour you should wear your most comfortable shoes. From **Piazza Giuseppe Poggi** we climb the stairs (*rampe*) to **Piazzale Michelangelo** (Bus No 13 will also take you there), providing one of the finest views of the entire city. Beyond town you can see the hills around Fiesole and Settignano and on a clear day the peaks of the Apuan Alps are visible to the west. On Sundays the square is transformed into a meeting place for youngsters on motorcycles, families with baby carriages, daddies buying balloons, boys on skateboards, not to mention the ubiquitous tourists.

Further on up the hill we come to **San Miniato al Monte**. The church (open 8am–noon and 2–7pm) owes its location to the fact that Saint Miniato, beheaded during the persecution of the Christians, was buried here in AD250. In 1013 a Benedictine abbey was erected here, soon followed by the current church which was completed in 1207. During the siege of Florence, Michelangelo protected its *campanile* (belltower) with mattresses against the stone cannonballs of the Imperial army. In 1553 the church was transformed into a fortress.

During the 17th century it was used as a hospital for victims of the plague, then later as a hospice for the homeless. The geometric marble exterior is a typical example of Florentine Romanesque style, whereas the interior reveals an unusual arrangement influenced by Byzantine models.

Next we stroll along shady **Viale Michelangelo**, created in the 19th century by the urban planner and architect Giuseppe Poggi during the period when Florence was the capital of Italy. The **Café Fontana**, once a well-known

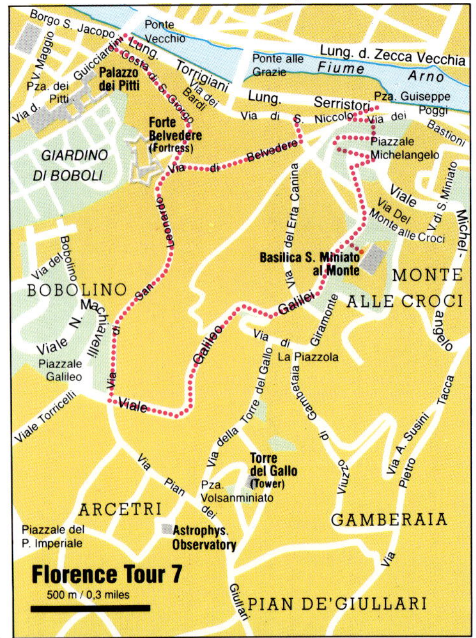


**Florence Tour 7**

500 m / 0,3 miles

*View from Piazzale Michelangelo*

artists' haunt, is a good place to rest for a while over a drink.

Having caught our breath, we turn into narrow **Via di S Leonardo** (beware of pickpockets on mopeds!) where many famous personalities have lived and where one still finds the most beautiful villas in Florence – surrounded by olive groves and yet only 10 minutes from the centre of the city. You can judge the hospitality and openness of the Florentines by the height of the walls isolating their villas from the outside world. On the right side at No 19, you will find the small church of **S Leonardo in Arcetri** (only open Sunday) with a marble pulpit going back to the 13th century.

Walking on, we come to the spectacular **Forte Belvedere** (open 8am–8pm) and its surrounding grounds. This fortress was constructed by the architect Buontalenti between 1590 and 1595, ostensibly for the defence of the city and of the Palazzo Pitti – then the residence of the Grand Duke – directly below. Actually, the fortress served to fend off danger not only *to* the city, but also *from* the city. One need not be a military strategist to imagine

*View from Forte Belvedere*

the advantages of its view of the city, lying at the foot of the fortress, in terms of suppressing possible uprisings. Each corner of the ramparts affords a totally different view: either of the city, of the hills or of the Boboli Gardens below.

Arriving back at the bottom, we turn left, passing through the **Porta S Giorgio**. This is the oldest city gate still standing (built in 1260) and it has a copy of a 13th-century carving of St George in combat with a dragon on its outer face (the original is now in the Palazzo Vecchio). Turn left and follow steep **Costa di S Giorgio**. When Galileo Galilei lived here, he used to walk down Via S Leonardo in the opposite direction to reach his observatory in Arcetri. We arrive at **Piazza Santa Felicita** (the church of the same name features works by Pontormo) and **Via de' Guicciardini** to realise, suddenly, that we are already back in the centre of the city.

Another option upon arriving at the Porta S Giorgio is to turn into small, rural **Via di Belvedere** and walk down to Via San Miniato. On your right you will come across a pleasant old café with tables outside. Alternatively, you can have an ice-cream at the **Latteria Frilli** (Via San Miniato) or a glass of wine and a bite to eat at the **Mescita Osteria San Niccolo** (Via San Niccolo No 60), located in the San Niccolo' area, which has managed to preserve its old character.

You can wander back to the Ponte Vecchio along the embankments of the Arno, or look out for the Via dei Bari, one step in from the river, a street lined with noble but austere 14th-century palaces, adorned with the coats of arms of their original owners.

# TUSCANY

## TOUR 1



**Through the Chianti region from castle to castle. With a length of 125 miles (200km), the tour can easily be covered in two days. To reach a few of the more remote highlights, some of the shorter stretches are along unpaved roads. And as far as where to stay: how about spending the night in a real monastery or castle?**

Without visiting this wine-growing area nobody can claim to have been to Tuscany. In this ordered and harmonious, gentle yet austere landscape one finds all the elements characteristic of the Florentine Renaissance – the sense of balance and proportion, for example. You will also begin to realise how the Tuscan spirit was shaped by this hard yet fertile earth. Situated between Florence and Siena in the heart of Tuscany, the **Chianti region** derives its name from the famous wine: grown in an area covering some 70,000 hectares (175,000 acres), chianti is sold by 800 wine-growing estates. We are going to visit a few

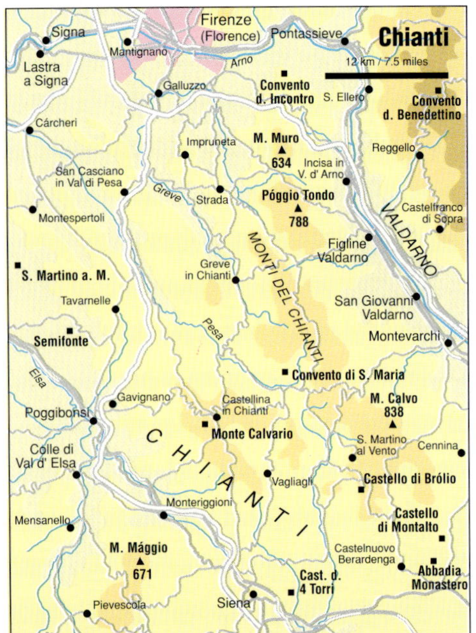

*Chianti landscape*

of them today, to experience the Tuscan landscape with its vineyards and olive groves, with its castles, abbeys and villas. Today 'Chiantishire' is a truly cosmopolitan world: the English, Americans, Germans and Dutch began to settle down here long ago – joined by Italians who can no longer bear living in the cities of Milan or Florence. Who is not familiar with chianti, one of the most famous wines in the world? But who knows that the name is derived from the Etruscan family name *Clante* and that even the Etruscans knew the wine – although today's chianti is made according to a recipe created by the 'Iron Baron', Bettino Ricasoli (one third sangiovese grapes, one third canaiolo, one third malvasia).

Well, then, let us get under way: starting at **Piazza Ferrucci** in Florence we follow the signs to **Greve** or **Siena**. Beyond the town of Grassina, typical Chianti landscape spreads out before us. To the left of the road watch for the lawns of the **Ugolino Golfclub** with an 18-hole course (Via Chiantigiana Impruneta 3, Phone: 055-2301009). Just the other side of **Strada** we take a left toward **Cintóia**. Already we can see the first medieval castle, the **Castello e Fattoria di Mugnana** (Phone: 055-858021). It goes back to the period of the Lombards and is one of the regions best-preserved castles. Here you also have the opportunity to taste and/or purchase your first Chianti wine. After a few more kilometres we arrive at the **Castello di Cintóia**, a Lombardic watchtower which is mentioned in records as early as AD996. If you look at the

*A quiet spot*

adjacent hill, you will see the late medieval **Sezzate Castle**. A couple of hundred metres on you will find a gushing spring, on the right, with very good drinking water. On the left-hand side we see a riding stable, Il Poderino.

Having passed through the small town of **La Panca** (where there is a broom festival in June) we drive to the left and up the hill to **Badia Montescalari**. A word of warning: the road is unpaved and rather bumpy. We arrive at a fork: around the curve to the right there is a beautiful *casa colonica* (typical farmhouse) with a church; heading on we reach Montescalari, a former monastery belonging to the Vallombrosan Order and going back to the 10th or 11th century. Today, a millennium later, you can spend the night in a monastic cell and dine in the refectory (tel: 055-959596). Up here there is a very pretty view of the surrounding hills.

The SP16 takes us to the main road, where we head left toward Ponte agli Stolli/Figline and, after about four kilometres, reach the lovely village of **Dudda** which, judging by the Roman graves that have been discovered here, is most likely of Roman origin.

Not far from Dudda we visit the **Castello di Querceto** (tel: 055-8549064), originally a Lombardic castle, which was largely rebuilt after its destruction in 1530. Here you can sample not only red, but also white wine, *vinsanto* (sweet dessert wine) and *aquavite* (spirits). I recommend, however, that you do not try everything at the same time!

If the weather is clear it is worth driving up **Monte S Michele** (elevation: 893m/2929ft) where you can see a long way out over the whole region. Passing through **Lucolena**, a small sleepy village, we head on to **Badia** (or Badiáccia) **a Montemuro**, another typical village complete with an *osteria* (rustic restaurant). This marks the beginning of the unpaved stretch of our trip. Next we reach **Albola**, a village known as early as AD1010 but scarcely inhabited today. From here on it's downhill, through vineyards.

Next we follow the main road ss429 to **Radda**, one of the main centres of the Chianti region. This pretty town in the middle of wine-growing country is surrounded by a wall. We park outside and follow the main road to Piazza Francesco Ferrucci and from there to the Palazzo del Podestà across from the church of San Nicola. You can taste and buy wine at the **Enoteca della Fattoria Vigna Vecchia** wine shop, 300 metres from Piazza Dante Alighieri. On the final Monday of each month a market is held in Radda. For lunch I recommend the welcoming **Villa Miranda** with its typical Tuscan atmosphere.

After a strong *espresso* to fight off afternoon drowsiness, we head past the Villa Bistarenni Strozzi, back down the same road we came (approximately 10km/6 miles) to **Badia a Coltibuono**, an enchanting wine estate set in a former abbey and monastery which goes back to the 8th century. If you did not dine in Miranda, the abbey restaurant now offers you an opportunity to do so (try the *grappa*). On the way back you can stop in at the estate shop and stock up with wine, oil, *grappa*, vinegar, *vinsanto* and honey.

*Badia Montescalari*

We now head for the tiny, marvellously renovated village of **Vertine**, then turn off the N408 to Castello Meleto, the **Meleto Fortress** (with an 18th-century theatre and adjoining wine estate) which was frequently attacked because of its border location between Florence and Siena. Turning left 3km (2 miles) further down the road, our next fortress is **Brolio**, the home of the inventor of Chianti, Baron Bettino Ricasoli. Regular tours are available (9–noon and 3pm–sunset); or consider buying wine and oil from his estate (tel: 0577-749710).

We drive back to the N408 and take a brief look at the Romanesque church of **S Giusto delle Monache**. We are now just outside Siena.

If you want to avoid the city traffic, you can take a route by way of Pontignano — otherwise take the N408 along the periphery of Siena and then follow the SS222 toward Castellina in Chianti.

Five kilometres (3 miles) after the wine-producing hamlet of **Fonterutoli** you will come to **Castellina** (whose centre is blocked off to traffic), a town which, as its name says, was originally conceived as a *castello*, a fortified castle. This castle was meant to be part of a larger Florentine defence system stretching from the Elsa Valley to the Arno Valley. Further evidence of these plans is the castle in the town centre, known as the **Rocca**. After admiring the medieval defences, consider investigating the wines in the nearby Bottega del Vino Gallo Nero (Via della Rocca 10) or perhaps dining in the rustic Antica Trattoria La Torre (Piazza del Comune; tel: 0577-740236).

Following the medieval Via delle Volte, we head back in the direction of Greve in Chianti. First, however, make another stop in **Panzano** with its churches Il Vinaio del Chianti and Santa Novella. The most impressive visual feature is its irregular Piazza G Matteotti lined with arcades. Here you will find culinary delights and interesting crafts: ham and salami at the **Antica Macelleria Falorni**, ice cream at the **Gelateria Lepanto** or carvings at the **Bottega dell'Artigianato.**

You can buy *vino sfuso* (unbottled wine, at lower prices than bottled wine) at the **Azienda Agricola San Martino a Uzzano** (Piazzetta S Croce 47) or else wait until **Uzzano** another 2km (1¼ miles) down the road – where you can buy it directly from the producers (*see page 55*).

Our final stop this side of Florence is **Impruneta**, whose main attraction is a very pretty pilgrimage church.

## Hotels

### HOTEL VILLA MIRANDA
*La Villa – Gaiole in Chianti*
*Tel: 0577-738021*
Doubles: 80,000–140,000 lire
Ms Miranda is a local celebrity: guests are pampered with Tuscan food and wine before bed in the cosy former post house.

### CASTELLO DI SPALTENNA
*Gaiole in Chianti*
*Tel: 0577-749483*
Doubles: 200,000–350,000 lire; Apartments: 400,000 lire
A renovated monastery with a Romanesque parish church. Restaurant in former refectory.

### LOCANDA BORGO ANTICO
*Lucolena – Greve in Chianti*
*Tel: 055-851024*
Doubles: 60,000 lire
Inn (and restaurant) beyond Lucolena, surrounded by hills.

### RELAIS BORGO SAN FELICE
*San Felice – Castelnuovo Berardenga*
*Tel: 0577-359260*
Doubles: 220,000–330000 lire
A well-known wine-growing estate: rooms are located in a medieval *case colonica* (farmhouse) in an atmospheric landscape.

### RESIDENCE VILLA CATIGNANO
*Catignano, Castelnuovo Berardenga*
*Tel: 0577-356755*
A beautiful villa with a view.

### IL COLOMBAIO
*Villa Ugurgeri della Berardenga Quercegrossa (10km/6 miles from Siena*
*Tel: 0577-52450*
Doubles: 100,000 lire
This is the family house of Count Ugurgeri della Berardenga; guests at Il Colombaio are served their meals in the Countess's dining room.

### TENUTA DI RICAVO
*Ricavo – Castellina in Chianti*
*Tel: 0577-740221*
Doubles: 180–360,000 lire
This country estate includes a *casa colonica* (farmhouse) and a swimming pool. For dining, evening dress is desirable.

### VILLA LE BARONE
*Via San Leolino 19*
*Panzano in Chianti*
*Tel: 055-852621*
Doubles 150,000–220,000 lire
This 16th-century villa is owned by a descendant of della Robbia. Swimming pool.

### ALBERGO GIOVANNI DA VERRAZZANO
*Piazza Matteotti 28*
*Greve in Chianti*
*Tel: 055-853189*
Doubles: 100,000 lire
This albergo has the advantage of a very central location on the beautiful piazza.

## Restaurants

**VILLA MIRANDA**
*La Villa – Gaiole in Chianti*
*Tel: 0577-738021*
Closed Tuesday. Tuscan dishes.

**BOTTEGA DEL 30**
*Villa a Sesta, near Castelnuovo*
*Baradenga*
*Tel: 0557-359226*
Closed Tuesday and Wednesday.
In the summer you can dine out-
doors. Large selection of wines.

**TRATTORIA DEL PELLEGRINO**
*Via del Chianti 30–34*
*Castelnuovo*
*Baradenga*
*Tel: 0557-355282*
Tuscan and standard Italian fare,
including pizzas.

**ALBERGACCIO DI CASTELLINA**
*Via Fiorentina 35*
*Castellina in Chianti*
*Tel: 0557-741042*
Closed Sunday and for lunch
Tuesday to Thusday. A former
barn. Charcoal-grilled meat and
homemade sausages.

**OSTERIA DI FONTERATOLI**
*Fonterutoli – Castellina in*
*Chianti*
*Tel: 0557-740212*
Closed Tuesday.

Typical Tuscan *osteria*. The specialities are game, stuffed rabbit
and homemade sausages.

**BADIA A COLTIBUONO**
*Between Radda and Gaiole*
*Tel: 0577-749424/749031*
Spit-roasted meats, tasty torelloni
in a charming abbey restaurant.
Closed Monday. Fairly pricey.

**VIGNALE**
*Via XX Settembre 23*
*Radda in Chianti*
*Tel: 0577-738094*
Rustic dishes served in a con-
verted farm building (a former
olive press). Expensive.

**IL VESCOVINO**
*Via Ciampolo da Panzano 9*
*Panzano in Chianti*
*Tel: 055-852464*
Closed Tuesday.
Terrace with panorama. Very
good cuisine. The building goes
back to the 14th century.

**IL VINAIO DEL CHIANTI**
*(next to the church)*
*Panzano in Chianti*
*Tel: 055-852603*
Closed Tuesday.
Bar, wine-tasting, live music;
vine-covered terrace with a view.

## Wine and Shopping

Although it is worth calling in
at any wine estate that appeals,
most estates prefer you to telephone in advance, particularly if
a tasting is required. You will
find the best wine at the following addresses:

**FATTORIA DI MUGNANA**
*Cintoia*
*Volpaia*
*Radda in Chianti*

**BADIA A COTTIBUONO**
*Between Radda and Gaiole (see page 51)*

**CASTELLO DI CACCHIANO**
*Gaiole in Chianti*
*Tel: 0577-747081*

**FATTORIA DI FONTERUTOLI**
*Fonterutoli*
*Tel: 055-852005 before visiting.*
Sells wine, honey, olive oil and lavender.

**CASTELLO IN VILLA**
*Castelnuovo Berardenga*
*Tel: 0577-359074 before visiting.*

**CASTELLARE**
*Castellina in Chianti*
*Tel: 0577-740490 before visiting.*

**CASTELLO DI RENCINE**
*Castellina in Chianti*
*Tel: 0577-743049 before visiting.*

**FONTODI**
*Panzano in Chianti*
*Tel: 055-852005 before visiting.*

**CASTELLO DI UZZANO**
*Greve in Chianti*
*Tel: 055-854032 before visiting.*

**VILLA CAFAGGIO**
*Panzano in Chianti*
*Tel: 055-8549090*

**ENOTECA**
*Greve in Chianti*
*Tel: 055-853297*
Specialised wine shop in Piazzetta Santa Croce, the town centre.

To go with the wine, buy a real *pecorino* (or *ricotta*) from **Gigi the Shepherd** (to find him, turn left 2 km/1½ miles beyond Lu-carelli, at Radda in Chianti). For ham, try **Macelleria Falorni**, Piazza Matteotti, Greve in Chianti.

## Special Events

**Chiocchio**
APRIL: Sagra del cinghiale
(Wild boar festival)

**Panzano in Chianti**
APRIL: Festa della stagione buona
(Spring festival)

**Greve in Chianti**
EASTER MONDAY: Mostra mercato di piante e fiori
(Flower show and market)

**S Polo in Chianti**
MAY: Festa del giaggiolo
(Iris festival)

**La Panca**
JUNE: Festa della ginestra
(Broom festival)

**Greve in Chianti**
SEPTEMBER: Mostra Mercato Vino Chianti Classico
(Chianti Classico wine-growers' festival in the capital of Chianti)

**Strada in Chianti**
SEPTEMBER: Antica Fiera
(Old-fashioned fair, with food and wine)

**Lucolena**
OCTOBER: Festa delle castagne
(Chestnut festival)

## Maremma

**On foot, on horseback or by kayak through the nature reserve, Parco Naturale della Maremma; to the villages in the interior; a day of relaxation on the Argentario with its brilliant blue lake. 150 miles (250km). Three days.**

This excursion is divided into three parts but you can give one segment preference over another. Bring bottled water and a picnic for Day 1.

'Bitter Maremma' it is called in one folksong. This marshland is famous for its horsebreeding, wild boar hunting and the austere villages of the interior. (Warning: in July there are *serafiche*, tiny insects whose bite is painful.) Today the land is very fertile in Maremma; even the Etruscans won extensive agricultural land by developing an ingenious irrigation system. The Maremma cattle, with their broad horns, are raised by *butteri* – real cowboys with strange leather trousers.

The Maremma region is popular among Italians but rarely visited by foreigners – yet. Maremman cuisine is highly praised and rightfully so, as you will experience for yourself. Vetulonia and Roselle, those important Etruscan excavation sites, are also located in this region.

**Maremma and Argentario**

8 km / 5 miles

*Tyrrhenian Sea*

*The swampy landscape of the Maremma*

**Day One:** We will spend the first day in the **Parco Naturale della Maremma** (Alberese, Ufficio Informazioni; tel: 0564-407098 because opening times vary according to the season and section visited). Covering around 60 square km (150 sq. miles) this nature park is full of wildlife, including wild boar, badgers, weasels and foxes. Birds of prey and water fowl are seen in large numbers and – beware – vipers, as well. The northern part of the park consists of beach, the southern portion is steep coastline. A variety of outings are possible: on foot (including guided tours in English in summer), on horseback or by kayak.

Passing Maremma cows on the bumpy road from Marina di Alberese, you reach the large 6-km/4-mile stretch of beach of Albarese – which is only crowded at the weekend in July or August. Parking is available and there are picnic sites with tables in the shade of pine trees. We can spend the night in **Talamone** (18km/11 miles from Alberese; the only accommodation being privately rented rooms), a small, still fairly picturesque harbour below the park – and our starting point for the next day. In Talamone itself you can climb to the top of the mountain and visit the harbour.

**Day Two:** Taking the road through San Donato (Etruscan grave of Aurelia, to the left of the Grosseto/Rome superstrada) we drive to **Magliano di Toscana**. On the way you will come across various Etruscan gravesites and the ruins of Romanesque churches. Perched above an olive orchard, Magliano is a fortified medieval village, established in the 11th century. The Palazzo dei Priori (1430, Siennese style), the Romanesque church of San Martino and the Gothic-Romanesque church of San Giovanni Battista are worth seeing.

The next stop after another 8km (5 miles) is charming **Pereta** where you should stretch your legs. If you have developed an appetite, you can have lunch in the restaurant **Wilma**. After another 10 km (6 miles) of hilly countryside we reach **Scansano** with its narrow alleyways and steep stairs in the old part of town.

Next we drive to the popular and typically Tuscan town of **Montemerano** (21km/13 miles). Here there is a ring of walls going back to the 15th century and the church of San Giorgio, 1430, with frescoes and a panel painting. Soon after, coming to a left-hand bend, you will see the waterfall of the thermal baths of **Saturnia**. You will find thermal swimming pools in the hotel Terme di Saturnia.

Stiff from all the driving, you can soak your aching limbs in the warm, soothing mineral solution. The ancients believed Saturnia to be the oldest settlement in Italy, which is why they gave it the divine name.

There is an Etruscan necropolis near Puntone, but the graves just before you get to Sovana are more worthwhile. Passing between flocks of sheep and herds of cattle, along steep slopes of red tufa, we continue to the **Temple Tomb of Ildebranda the Etruscan**. A three-minute walk from the road, it is something you should not miss.

Passing through a tunnel the road takes us to the very beautiful, although heavily visited, town of **Sovana** (15½ miles/ 25km; SP22; up to the right). In this little tufa-stone jewel we should not pass up a visit to the proto-Romanesque church. Back on the main road, heading on past the Villa Orsini another kilometre, we come to a left turn to **Sorano**, which is situated above a deep ravine with a roaring stream and a waterfall. If there is no time left for this small medieval village, then take a right turn to a truly impressive place: **Pitigliano** (6 km/4 miles) with the oldest Italian synagogue, the Palazzo Orsini (14th-century) and the tufa caves which are used as cellars for the local white wine – this you should drink in the company of genuine Pitiglians at Via Roma 53.

Continuing through the hilly landscape we reach **Manciano** and lovely **Capálbio** before crossing the Via Aurélia, and then on to **Lago di Burano**. If we are in luck and arrive by sundown, we will be able to witness a tremendous show. Depending on the time of year, flocks of migrating birds stop over here. The lagoon has been placed under the protection of the World Wildlife Fund (guided tours outside the breeding season). Before the sun has entirely set we drive on via Ansedonia to Monte Argentario.

**Day Three: Monte Argén-tario** was once an island, but there are now three causeways connecting it to the mainland. This massif with a circumference of 40km (25 miles) reaches an elevation of 635 me-tres (2,000ft). Mediter-ranean *macchia*, olive groves and vineyards prevail as green vege-tation. Except in Porto Santo Stefano there has been hardly any speculative building here.

The coastline here is extremely varied, but unfortunately rather inaccessible for most people. 'Private' is the catchword, for this is one of the romping grounds, between Rome and Milan, favoured by the jet set due to the initiative of the mayor, Susanna Agnelli, Italy's Foreign Minister and the Fiat tycoon's sister.

Of the two towns, **Porto Santo Stefano** and **Porto Ercole,** the latter is the prettier; it features a castle and a Spanish fortress. Behind Porto Ercole the coast turns back into rocky cliffs with small coves. For several kilometres the road becomes almost impassable unless you have a four-wheel drive jeep – but if you are not worried about the underside of your car you will be rewarded by a lovely landscape.

The road becomes paved again just before reaching **Cala Piccola**, a pleasant holiday village complete with hotel, and from there on

to Porto Santo Stefano. Two of the few beaches which do not require great effort to reach are **La Cannelle** (approximately opposite Isola Rossa) and the beach to the left of the luxury hotel Il Pellicano, a couple of kilometres past Porto Ercole.

To really enjoy Argentario you would have to stay in a pretty hotel with a private beach, or else visit the peninsula off-season, when strolling through town is more popular than swimming. Not that the sea is not lovely. It is wonderful but, as I said, very inaccessible – except from a yacht.

The small **Island of Giglio** is pretty with its inviting bathing beach of Campese. It can be reached daily by ferry from Porto Santo Stefano (in the summer by hydrofoil).

## Practical Information

Many hotels here insist on half or full board. Prices given below are for two people sharing a double room.

## Hotels

**HOTEL CORTE DEI BUTTERI**
*Aurelia – 156km (Grosseto)*
*Tel: 0564-885548*
Double: 300,000–640,000 lire
Open April to mid-October.

**HOTEL CAPO D'UOMO**
*Via Cala di Forno*
*Talamone*
*Tel: 0564-887077*
Double: 150,000 lire
Situated on a cliff-top overlooking the sea.

**VILLA DOMIZIA**
*Loclità 5 Liberata*
*Porto Santo Stefano*
*Tel: 0564-812735*
Full board: 300,000 lire. Modern villa with panoramic views and terrace restaurant.

**LOCANDA LAUDOMIA**
*Poderi di Montemerano*
*Tel: 0564-620062*
Double: 80,000 lire
View of the hills; very good cuisine (pricey).

**HOTEL LE TERME DI SATURNIA**
*Ristorante Villa Montepaldi*
*Club Benessere*
*Saturnia*
*Tel: 0564-601061*
Full board: 500,000 lire.

Luxury hotel. You can use the thermal pool and treatments without staying in the hotel.

**HOTEL VILLA CLODIA**
*Via Italia 43*
*Saturnia*
*Tel: 0564-601212*
Double: 110,000 lire
Central location. Lovely view and swimming pool.

**ALBERGO TAVERNA ETRUSCA**
*Piazza del Pretorio 16*
*Sovana*
*Tel: 0564-616183*
Double: 80,000 lire
On the main square of Sovana. Certain dishes are prepared at the fireplace under the eyes of the hungry guests.

**TORRE DI CALAPICCOLA**
*Cala Piccola – Monte Argentario*
*Tel: 0564-825144*
Apartment: 150,000–300,000 lire per person.
Open April to mid-October. Hotel in a tower, otherwise holiday apartments. Choice view of the adjacent island, Giglio.

**DON PEDRO**
*Via Panoramica 7*
*Porto Ercole*
*Tel: 0564-833914*
Full board: 350,000 lire.

**IL PELLICANO**
*Località Cala dei Santi*
*Sbarcatello – Porto Ercole*
*Tel: 0564-833801*
Double: 400,000–610,000 lire; full board: 1000,000 lire.
Open Easter to October.
Exclusive, tennis and pool.

## Restaurants

**TRATTORIA DA WILMA**
*Via Roma*
*Pereta*
*Tel: 0564-908079*
Closed Thursday.
Top home-style cooking.

**CAINO**
*Via della Chiesa 4*
*Montemerano*
*Tel: 0564-602817*
Closed Wednesday. Very good.

**DUE CIPPI-DA MICHELE**
*Piazza Vittorio Veneto 26*
*Saturnia*
*Tel: 0564-601074*
Maremman dishes served in a patrician palazzo. Reserve.

**TAVERNA ETRUSCA**
*Piazza del Pretorio 16*
*Sovana*
*Tel: 0564-616183*
Closed Monday.
Local specialities are prepared before guests in a medieval dining room – one of the most exclusive restaurants in Maremma.

IL CAVALLINO
*Via Baschieri 36*
*Porto Santo Stefano*
*Tel: 0564-817649*
Closed Monday.
Fish is the speciality of the house.

IL GAMBERO ROSSO
*Lungomare Andrea Doria 70*
*Porto Ercole*
*Tel: 0564-832650*
Closed Wednesday.
Terrace with a view. Maremman and fish dishes. Pricey.

PUNTO D'INCONTRO
*(Restaurant/piano bar)*
*Cala Galera – Porto Ercole*
*Tel: 0564-832032*
Open every day during the summer; weekends only during the winter. Very trendy.

## Discos

KING LIDO DISCOTHEQUE
*Bar-Ristorante*
*Cala-Galera – Porto Ercole*
*Tel: 0564-833912*
Open every day from June to September; Friday and Saturday only during the winter.

## Shopping

IL FRANTOIO ANDREINI
*Via Amiatina 25*
*Poggioferro (Scansano)*
Maremma delicacies.

MAREMMA MAGLIA
*Via Italia*
*Montemerano*
Handmade wool and cotton sweaters in pretty colours.

MONS AMERANUS
*Via Italia*
*Montemerano*
Antiques.

ASTANTE
*Piazza Vittorio Veneto*
*Saturnia*
Knitwear, suitcases, straw goods.

MIELE
*Piazza Vittorio Veneto*
*Saturnia*
Honey, sold by the producer.

MARCO VINCENTI
*Via del Duomo 17*
*Sovana*
Antiques.

## Special Events

**Grosseto**
**1–3 MAY** and **15 AUGUST**
*Torneo dei Butteri*
Horseback games: the players try to steal roses pinned on each other's costumes.

**Starting with Boccaccio's house; the medieval City of Towers, S Gimignano; to Volterra and into the Colline Metallifere, the 'metal-bearing hills'; Massa Marittima and the abandoned abbey of S Galgano. 150 miles (250km). A relaxed two-day trip.**

*Certaldo, come voi forse avete potuto udire, è un Castel di Val d'Elsa.*
*Certaldo, as you must have heard, is a castle in the Valley of Elsa.*

**Boccaccio**, *Decameron*

To reach Certaldo (Certaldo Alto) from Florence you follow the *superstrada* in the direction of Siena, taking the S Donato and Tavarnelle Val di Pisa exit. Poggibonsi is an alternative exit. The first route, however, passes through more scenic landscape. There is plenty of parking available by the Palazzo Pretorio.

Born in Paris, Boccaccio also lived for some time in the red-brick city of **Certaldo**. He died here and was buried in the church of SS **Michele and Jacopo** (13th century; both the exterior and interior are brick masonry, with della Robbia terracotta figures).

Boccaccio's house, where he also died, is open to the public and is worth visiting (**Casa del Boccaccio**, Via Boccaccio; open 9am–noon and 3–6pm). This small town palazzo has a distinctly patrician air. It is quite an experience, especially its small rooms and its steep and narrow staircases. In fact, the overall austerity and dignity suggests anything but the excesses we associate with Boccaccio's stories. We may presume that it was in the upper, more airy loggia that Boccaccio wrote his later works.

Certaldo still looks the same as the poet knew it back then: a small world where time has stood still. You can readily imagine

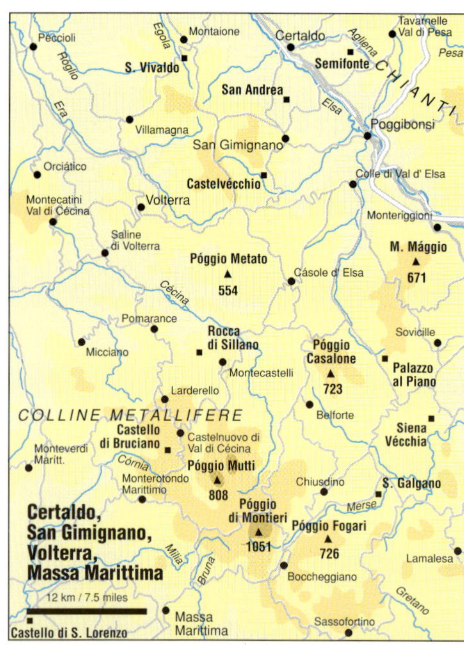

*Rural landscape*

yourself in a totally different century: seeing a smiling Monna Something with a jug on her head stepping out of a house… If only such daydreams were not always abruptly interrupted by the nervous honking of some car.

Walking up the narrow alleyway to its end, you will discover the **Palazzo Pretorio** looming over the town. In its original form it dates back to the 13th century; it was then reconstructed during the 15th century and now houses a small museum. In the **Loggia** to the far right the Court pronounced its verdicts. Other points of interest are the courtroom, the inner courtyard and the dungeon with the graffiti of former inmates. From the rooms there is a view of red roofs and vineyards. It is now high time for a fortifying breakfast on the terrace of a former monastery, **Osteria del Vicario** (Via Rivellino), before heading out of town again.

Putting another 14km (9 miles) behind us, we reach **San Gimignano** (you will not need the car to get around, so leave it at the parking lot outside the town wall). With its tall towers and the double circle of walls, this is certainly the most impressive medieval city in Tuscany – the town where Florentine, Pisan and Sienese influences converged and mingled. Prior to 1580 the city boasted a grand total of 72 towers – today there are only 15. As well as defending the city, the towers served as status symbols. No private tower was ever allowed to exceed the height of the Podestà tower. In Florence as well as in other Tuscan city-states, as soon as the *popolani* (the middle class) had acquired sufficient power, they simply tore down the towers of the *magnati* (the city

*San Gimignano*

nobles). San Gimignano, however, lost its autonomy at an early stage – before it could smash the power of the nobility. This is the reason such a relatively large number of towers were left standing for us to admire today. You can climb to the top of **Torre Grossa**, the tallest tower in town. The **Collegiata** (church) contains an astonishing cycle of frescoes by Bartolo di Fredi as well as a frescoed chapel and an Annunciation by Ghirlandaio. The **Piazza del Duomo** with its uneven surface is the cheerful centre of the city. Directly next to it is the **Piazza della Cisterna** with its curious fountain. Today six towers line the square which, following the sloping contour of the hill, is neither plane nor perpendicular. From the **Rocca**, the fortress, there is a terrific view of the strange, surreal landscape, the so-called *Crete* region, named after the curious clay hummocks. Driving out of town – on your way to Volterra – stop to look back at a timeless view.

Thirteen kilometres (8 miles) down the road we reach the N68 and continue to **Volterra**. This last bastion of the Etruscans against the Romans is surrounded by an austere circular wall, a reminder that the city was constantly at war with San Gimignano. The centre of town is dominated by the **Palazzo dei Priori** (1208), the oldest town hall in Tuscany. Around the corner, on Via dei Sarti, is the **Pinacoteca** (open 10am–1pm and 3–6pm), a picture gallery with works by Signorelli and Ghirlandaio. Via Turrazzo leads to the Duomo (the medieval cathedral frescoed by Gozzoli) and to the octagonal baptistry.

Taking Via Roma off to the right you will reach **Casa Torre Buonparenti** with its Pisan appearance, dating back to the

*Piazza della Cisterna*

13th century. The tiny windows are amusing – they were designed with children in mind. Via Sari will lead you to the little S Michele Arcangelo church and to the **Casa-Torre Toscano** tower (13th-century). The fortress (1472) has been turned into a prison and before you insist on a tour, remember: getting in is much easier than getting out.

The climax of any visit to Volterra must undoubtedly be the important **Guarnacci Museum** containing Etruscan treasures which the archaeologist Mario Guarnacci began collecting as early as 1732 (Via Don Minzoni; open March to October 9am–1pm and 3–6.30pm; 10am–2pm rest of year). The Etruscans exploited the same alabaster deposits still being quarried today – they used this soft yellowish material to carve their burial urns. Looking at the lids of the urns today we see their mysterious expressions – the expressions of people whom nothing has surprised for centuries.

The only surviving example of Etruscan architecture, the **Arco Etrusco**, is overwhelming. From the **Porta Menseri** you look down into the abyss: the **balze** are a series of cliffs caused by erosion which have already swallowed up churches and almost pulled a monastery into the depths.

We next proceed in the direction of Pomarance and Massa (67km/40 miles). Taking the turn-off to Massa, and passing Saline, we enter the **Colline Metallifere**, the 'metal-bearing hills' that mark the northern margins of volcanic Italy. Geysers, sulphurous pools and strange pipelines may make you think you are in a science-fiction film. At the **Valle del Diavolo**, Devil's Valley, you may want to make a detour to **San Dalmazio** (5km/3 miles), a

*Group photo with pigeons*

charming, village, or drive a kilometre further to the ruins of a Romanesque church or an additional kilometre to the Gothic **S Dalmazio**.

Situated further up (45mins on foot) are **Rocca di Sillano** (11th century; excellent views!) and **Montecastelli** (Terme S Michele). Ignoring Larderello on the left (look out for geothermal facilities), we pass La Perla (thermal baths) and drive on through a landscape green with chestnut and oak trees – passing the fork (sp11) to the thermal baths on the left. Probably of Etruscan origin, Massa Marittíma was the birthplace of St Bernard and is located at the centre of the mining area. The Massa Mining Codex (1310), was the world's first legislative regulation for the mining industry.

Located on the asymmetrical cathedral square, we discover the

**Palazzo Pretorio** (13th-century) and the centre of this city, the 12th-century cathedral. Besides the cathedral's Romanesque reredos either by Duccio Buoninsegna or his school, it is worth taking a look at the Augustinian church (14th century) and the clocktower (1228).

Leaving Massa we drive back to the N441 – with S **Galgano** as our final destination. We still have another 35km (20 miles) to go, and we must see to it that we arrive by sunset or very early in the morning. There, on top of a green hill, is the big secret: a Cistercian abbey, with sky where the roof should be. Swallows fly in and out through the windows, the floor consists of grass and all around: nothing but silence. Once, as I arrived, I heard Gregorian chanting from afar. As I 'entered', the monks were singing under a canopy of blue sky.

## Practical Information

### Hotels

**OSTERIA DEL VICARIO**
*Via Rivellino 3, Certaldo Alto*
*Tel: 0571-668228*
Double: 180,000 lire
Terrace and restaurant with romantic cloisters.

**HOTEL LA CISTERNA**
*Piazza della Cisterna*
*San Gimignano*
*Tel: 0557-940328*
Double: 125,000 lire

**HOTEL BEL SOGGIORNO**
*Via San Giovanni 91*
*San Gimignano*
*Tel: 0557-940375*
Double: 115,000 lire
Medieval palazzo and panoramic restaurant.

**HOTEL PESCILE**
*Pescille—San Gimignano*
*Tel: 0577-940186*
Double: 115,000 lire
Panorama and swimming pool.

**CONVENTO DI SANT'AGOSTINO**
*Piazza Sant'Agostino*
*San Gimignano*
*Tel: 0577-940383*
Double: 40,000 lire
Write to Padre Superiore in advance if you want to stay in this monastery.

**VILLA NENCINI**
*Borgo S Stefano—Volterra*
*Tel: 0588-86386*
Double: 100,000 lire
An old villa with a view.

**ALBERGO IL SOLE**
*Via della Libertà 43*
*Massa Marittima*
*Tel: 0566-901971*
Double: 85,000 lire

## Restaurants

**DORANDO**
*Vicolo dell'Oro 2*
*San Gimignano*
*Tel: 0577-941862*
'Genuine' Etruscan food in an intimate palazzo.

**LE VECCHIE MURA**
*Via Piandornella*
*San Gimignano*
*Tel: 0577-940270*
Closed Tuesday.
The best in San Gimignano.

**LA TAVERNETTA**
*Via Guarnacci 14*
*Volterra*
*Tel: 0588-87630*
Closed Thursday.
Especially good game and mushrooms.

**IL VECCHIO BORGO**
*Via Parenti 12*
*Massa Marittima*
*Tel: 0566-903950*
Closed Sunday evenings and Monday. Inexpensive.
Venison or truffle *crostini*.

**OSTERIA**
*Vicolo Porte*
*Massa Marittima*
*Tel: 0566-901991*
Closed Tuesday. Pleasing, rustic ambience.

**DA SBRANA**
*Ghirlanda—Massa Marittima*
*Tel: 0566-902704*
Closed Monday.
In the mountains.

**BRACALI**
*Ghirlanda—Massa Marittima*
*Tel: 0566-902063*
Culinary speciality: boar. Gentrified rustic style.

## Shopping

**ARAZZI DA INDOSSARE**
*Via XX Septembre 2*
*San Gimignano*
Handwoven goods.

**LA CERAMICA IN SILIVA BEGHE**
*Via San Mateo*
*San Gimignano*

**AZIENDA AGRICOLA TOLLENA**
*Via San Giovanni 71*
*San Gimignano*
Panoramic view from patio.
Place for Vernaccia wine.

## Museums and Monuments

**Palazzo Pretorio**
*Certaldo Alto*
The museum inside can be visited by appointment only, tel: 0571-661259/664208.

**PINACOTECA CIVICO (MUSEO CIVICO)**
*San Gimignano*
Summer: 9.30am–7pm. Winter: 9.30am–5.30pm. Closed Monday. Fabulous collection of Florentine and Sienese masterpieces, including madonnas by Benozzo Gozzoli.

Museo d'Arte Sacra
*San Gimignano*
Summer: 9.30am–7pm. Winter:
9.30am–5.30pm. Has religious
paintings and Etruscan artefacts.

Teatro Romano
*Viale Ferrucci, Volterra*
Roman theatre just outside the
city walls. Market held here on
Saturday mornings.

Palazzo del Podestà
*Pinacoteca/Museo Archeologico*
*Piazza Garibaldi*
*Massa Marittima*
Open 10am–1pm and 3– 5pm.
Closed on Monday.

Museo della Miniera
*Massa Marittima*
Open: April to September,
10am–12.30am and 3.30–7pm;
October to March, 11am–1pm
and 4–5pm. Guided tours every
half hour.

## Special Events

**Volterra**
July: *Volterra Teatro* – Theatre
festival on Piazza dei Priori.
July/August: Crossbow tour-
nament, Piazza de Priori.
**First Sunday in September**:
Flag throwing.

**Massa Marittima**
A Sunday around 20 May and
again on the feast of St Bernard
in the middle of August: *Balestro
del Girafalco* – flag throwing
and crossbow tournament.
July to 20 September: *Mercato
dell'Artigianato* – crafts market.

## Pisa, Lucca and the Garfagnana

**Pisa and the Leaning Tower (see it while it is still standing);
Lucca; ascent into the remote and undeveloped Garfagnana region
and the Apuan Alps; to Carrara. This is a two-day trip with
options given for extending it to a week.**

Pisa's **Piazza del Duomo** is better known by the name of 'Campo
dei Miracoli', the Miracle Field. The buildings seem to shoot out
of the grass, as if by some miracle: the gleaming Cathedral, the
Baptistry, the Camposanto and the Leaning Tower – all enclosed
by the old city wall. I recommend you rest on the grass and take
your time studying the façade – the quintessence of Pisan ecclesiastical
architecture (providing, that is, that the grass is not so packed that
you will have to worry about being stepped on). Moving inside the
Duomo (closed 12.45–3pm), you will find a pulpit by Giovanni
Pisano. The realism in the rendering of the figures in the scenes

*The Piazza del Duomo in Pisa*

from the life of Christ is astounding. From the outside, the **Baptistry** lacks harmony due to the tremendous variety of detail. The interior, by contrast, radiates a simple elegance. The pulpit by Nicola Pisano is charged with such emotion that even the horses portrayed seem to weep.

The earth in the **Camposanto** (summer 8am–8pm, winter 9am–5pm), the cemetery with the white walls, was brought from Mount Calvary by returning Crusaders. The frescoes of the *Triumph Over Death* are shattering in their revelation of the macabre world of the medieval imagination. What a contrast to the landscape by Taddeo Gaddi. On the opposite side of the square you have the **Museo delle Sinopie** (open 9.30–12.40am and 3–6.40pm) with its collection of frescoes (*sinopie*) discovered during restoration work after World War II.

Is it still standing – really? Construction work on Pisa's **Tower** went on for nearly 200 years, because its deviant behaviour became only too apparent right from the start. Recently the tilt has increased but a project to stabilise the tilt at about 5 degrees off the perpendicular is underway. When it is finished, you should be able to climb all the way to the top and take in the wonderful view.

The **Museo dell'Opera del Duomo** (open 9am–1pm, 3–5pm) and the **Museo Nazionale di San Matteo** (open 9am–7pm, Sunday and holidays from 9am–1pm; closed Monday) are treasure troves of Pisan art. Heading along Via Santa Maria and Piazza San Felice, Via de Mille and Via Corsica you will reach **Piazza dei Cavalieri**, once the

*Garfagnana—untouched by tourism*

centre of activity in the Republic of Pisa. It was in one of the towers of the **Palazzo dell'Orologio** – so we learn from Dante's *Inferno* – that a certain Count Ugolino, wrongly convicted of treason, was allowed to starve to death together with his sons. Turning into Via dei Consoli del Mare we come to **Piazza Santa Caterina** and its eponymous church. The **Borgo Stretto** quarter is the Old Town and is full of narrow alleyways. Arriving at the beautiful Piazza delle Vettovaglie with its arcade we can stop in at the **Trattoria La Mescita** for a bite to eat. Walking across the Ponte di Mezzo and then along Lungarno Gambacorti will take us to the church of **Santa Maria della Spina**, a true gem of Pisan Gothic architecture (1230). Here, seafarers prayed before setting sail.

Opera fans on their way to Lucca can make the pilgrimage to **Torre del Lago Puccini**, to the Puccini villa on the Lake of Massaciuccoli to trace the *Tosca* composer's footsteps or attend the August Puccini festival. While at the lake, hungry opera-lovers will surely want to stop in at **Cecco** to try the excellent game specialities. If you choose this itinerary, do not take Road N12, the direct road (22km/14 miles) to Lucca. Instead follow the N1 (about 20km/12 miles) to the lake. From there the N439 (15km/10 miles) leads to **Lucca**.

The **Piazza Napoleone** is the lively centre of Lucca; you'll find it quieter on the **Piazza San Martino**, reached by way of Via del Duomo, where the asymmetrical **cathedral** seems to be leaning

*In the Apuan Alps*

on its *campanile* (belltower). Inside you will find works by Nicola Pisano, as well as the famous *Tomb of Ilaria del Carretto* by Jacopo della Quercia, one of the most significant achievements of Italian sculpture. There are also works by Tintoretto and Ghirlandaio.

Heading down Via del Duomo, you will reach the **Piazza San Michele** with its typical brick buildings, where the annual *Palio della Balestra*, a crossbow competition going back to feudal times, is held on 12 July. The church **San Michele in Foro** is in Pisan-Lucchese style with a holy picture by Lippi inside.

Afterwards, tired as we are, let us visit the former pharmacy **Massa** (Piazza San Michele) for a fortifying glass of wine. Alternatively, we can stop off on Via Fillungo for a *biadina* with pine nuts floating in it. This is served at the **Antico Caffè di Simo —** where any evening you can watch half of Lucca strolling by. A bit further on, at the Piazza Scarpellini, we can scrutinize the mummy of Saint Zita in the Romanesque church of **San Frediano**, where each 26 April she is taken out and celebrated. Next, our route takes us by way of the oval Piazza Anfiteatro (site of the ancient Roman amphitheatre) and Via A Mondoni onto **Via Guinigi**, where the medieval palazzi with their red brickwork and white marble columns are still well preserved. The tower of the Palazzo Guinigi offers a good view (summer: Monday to Saturday 9am–7.30pm; winter: 10am–4.30pm).

Winding up our tour, we can walk along the imposing city wall, gaining a different impression of Lucca (you can also do this stretch by bicycle: booked from the tourist office on Piazzale Verdi or from Casermetta Santa Croce, tel: 0583-587857).

If you happen to be travelling with children, you can take an interesting detour from Lucca, heading out on the N435 to **Collodi**, the birthplace of Pinocchio – where the life of that little wooden rogue is portrayed in a large theme park. Otherwise, you follow the N12 (8km/5 miles) out of Lucca until you take the turn-off to **Marlia**. Look for the royal **Villa Pecci-Blunt** with its gorgeous park at the foot of a hill, the site of a summer music festival. Among the guests of this villa were Niccolo Paganini and Prince Metternich.

The area is dotted with beautiful villas, known as the Ville Lucchesi.

This is the start of the **Garfagnana** region, stretching out on both sides of the River Serchio, between the Apuan Alps and the Apennines. This inaccessible and remote region was isolated from the rest of Tuscany for

*Ponte del Diavolo*

centuries and popular traditions long lost elsewhere have been preserved here. For example, the epic *maggi*, which originally welcomed the beginning of summer, are still performed, as are various Christmas plays and the *sacre rappresentazioni* at Easter. Don't expect tremendous works of art. Instead the region offers wild, unadulterated nature, as well as a cultural tradition all its own, presenting a different, unexpected face of Tuscany.

Back on the N2 we head in the direction of Borgo a Mozzano; coming up on the right there is a turn-off to the Romanesque church of **Pieve di Brancoli**. If you miss it, you can take a look at Pieve S Donato in **Domazzano** or the isolated Pieve di S Maria (13th century) in **Diecimo,** both to the left of the road on the other bank of the Serchio. Back on the road, once you have passed Borgo a Mozzano on the left bank of the Serchio, you will come to a bridge whose daring design is truly amazing: the **Ponte del Diavolo**. This strange construction goes back to the 14th century. A legend has it that the builder appealed to the Devil himself for assistance; Satan supposedly demanded the soul of the first to cross the bridge as payment. The bridge builder – the Pontifex – who made this pact with the Devil, tricked the Evil One. The first to cross the bridge was a dog – helped on its way by a swift kick up the backside from the Pontifex.

But let's hurry on, back across the river. It's another 7km (4 miles) on the N12, to **Bagni di Lucca**. In the 18th and 19th centuries, these old thermal baths were particularly popular among English poets because of the therapeutic effects of the warm, sulfurous waters. Shelley, Heine, Byron and the Brownings bathed here. The water seems to work wonders on paralysis.

From Bagni di Lucca there is a paved road to the picturesque, high-lying village of **Montefegatesi**, and from here you can reach the dreaded white-water gorge **Orrido di Botri**. There are two paths leading to the ravine: an easy trail from the parking lot (with nearby picnic grounds) and another from the **Rifugio Losentini**, which can only be recommended to very experienced mountaineering and climbing fanatics. Back on the N445 there is another temptation in store: **Coréglia Antelminelli**, surrounded by chestnut woods. Among other things, it includes a crafts museum. In addition, there are two churches, both Romanesque, **S Martino** (9th century) and **S Michele** (12th century).

*Calomini Cloister*

*Montefegatesi*

The next stop on our tour is the beautiful and fashionable city of **Barga.** Parking our car outside the city wall, we enter through the city gate and head to the left through the narrow, winding streets with their palazzi modelled after those in Florence. The historic **Bar Capretz** is where the city's *noblesse* has met for a cultivated chat ever since the end of the 18th century.

At the top of the hill we reach the peak of our visit to Barga: the 11th-century **SS Pietro e Paolo Cathedral**. Its treasures are an extraordinary pulpit, the Lombardic polychrome figure of St Christopher, alabaster windows and the terracotta figures by della Robbia in the Cappella del Sacramento. From up here there is a 360-degree view of the Garfagnana mountains.

Now for something completely different: on the opposite side of the Serchio there is a road leading 9km (5½ miles) along the Turrite brook to the well-known **Grotta del Vento** (Cave of the Wind) in the Apuan Alps, with 10,000ft (3,000m) of tunnels and caverns. The tour of the continuously changing grotto with its glorious colours takes a total of two hours. Assuming you don't suffer from claustrophobia, I think you will not regret the descent deep into this stony gulley.

On our way back – before reaching the main N445 – we turn left to make our way up to the **Calomini Cloister**, the home of a single friar, Frate Maurizio. Living here in solitude and silence, he shares this place only with the eagles and owls. What is the explanation for a Capuchin monastery clinging to this rocky slope in the middle of nowhere? Supposedly, around the year 1,000, a small girl was climbing up this mountain when she found a picture of the Madonna in a grotto. Once they heard about this, the village inhabitants hurried to take the relic to their own parish church – however, the Mother of God did not fancy this and the icon returned to the grotto. The lively Madonna repeated this stunt several times until

the peasants of Gallicano finally gave up and built a small church around the grotto.

Next we set out for **Castelnuovo di Garfagnana** where the poet Ludovico Ariosto spent three years as governor of Garfagnana. The **Rocca** is the most interesting site here. Next we have several options. It is unfortunate that we cannot do them all, unless you have a whole week.

The **first route** takes in: **Castelnuovo**, **Pieve Fosciana** (one of the oldest churches in Garfagnana), **San Pellegrino in Alpe** (shrine with a panoramic view and an interesting museum: 'Life in the Past'), **Sassorosso** (an atmospheric village of red stone from the nearby marble quarry), **Castiglione** (an impressive medieval village fortress), then turn left onto the N324 for **Carrara**.

The **second route** takes in **Pieve Fosciana**, **Castiglione**, **Villa Collemandina** (Romanesque church), **Corfino** (vacation and health resort at the foot of Pania di Corfino, elevation: 1,603metres/5,260ft) and then on to the **Parco dell'Orecchiella** (inquiries at the Centro Visitatori, tel: 0583-619098). The park is full of deer, chamois, wild boar, badgers, otters, weasels, eagles and buzzards, as well as 250 different types of flora. The return route is via to **Verrucole**, **S Romano** and especially impressive **Sambuca**.

The **third route** takes us from Castelnuovo along the N445 to **Poggio** near the beautiful and lonely church of **S Biagio** (1086). At Pon Poggio we take a left turn along a very beautiful stretch, to **Vagli di Sotto** and **Vagli di Sopra**, the oldest settlements in Garfagnana. In Vagli di Sotto the parish church of **S Regolo** is worth seeing. But the special attraction is the lake with the submerged village of **Fabbrica di Careggine** – more or less visible depending on the water level. Sometimes the lake dries up completely, entirely exposing the village.

Then we make our way back to Castelnuovo and then right along **Túrrite Secca** and along the Isola Santa lake (the church is in the water; sometimes you can see the tip of its steeple) towards **Arni**. Soon the so-called **Marmitte dei Giganti** ('giants' cooking pots') appear: 23 huge hollows (20m/65ft in diameter), a geological phenomenon. Some have steps for climbing in and out. Be careful: you do not want to wind up in the giants' soup.

The next leg of our journey is to the right to Arni, we then drive past the large marble quarries and on through the **Galleria del Cipollaio** carved out of the marble. From here the road leads down to **Seravezza** and **Forte dei Marmi**; an alternative route would take us from the Galleria to the right to **Massa** and **Carrara**.

### Hotels

**JOLLY HOTEL CAVALIERI**
*Piazza Stazione 2*
*Pisa*
*Tel: 050-43290*
Double: 350,000 lire.

**VILLA LA PRINCIPESSA**
*Massa Pisana (Lucca) ss12*
*Tel: 0583-370037*
Double: 310,000 lire. Closed January and February. Old patrician house renovated by the Bourbon-Parma.

**VILLA CASANOVA**
*Via di Casanova*
*Balbano (Lucca) SS12*
*Tel: 0583-548429*
Double: 95,000 lire. March to October. Rooms and apartments available. Halfway between Lucca and the sea: a working estate with vineyards and olive orchards selling its own produce.

**HOTEL HAMBROS**
*Banchieri – Lunata di Lucca*
*Tel: 0583-935355*
Double: 130,000 lire
Old villa situated 9km (5½ miles) from Lucca. The rooms to the rear are the quietest. Note: breakfast here is as expensive as lunch.

**ALBERGO VILLA LIBANO**
*Via del Sasso 6*
*Barga*
*Tel: 0583-723774*
Double: 75,000 lire

**HOTEL/RISTORANTE CARLINO**
*Via Garibaldi 15*
*Castelnuovo di Garfagnana*
*Tel: 0583-644270*
Double: 80,000 lire

## Restaurants

**LA MESCITA**
*Via Cavalca 2*
*Pisa*
*Tel: 050-544292*
Tuscan ambience. Closed Sunday.

**SERGIO**
*Lungarno Pacinotti 1*
*Pisa*
*Tel: 050-580580*
Medieval palazzo. Closed Sunday and Monday lunch. Pisan cuisine.

**DA GIULIO IN PELLERIA**
*Via delle Conci 47*
*Lucca*
*Tel: 0583-55948*
Closed Sunday and Monday. Reservations only; offbeat menu.

**ALL'OLIVO**
*Piazza S Quirico 1*
*Lucca*
*Tel: 0583-46264*
Swordfish is the house speciality.

**ANTICA LOCANDA DELL'ANGELO**
*Via Pescheria/Corte dell'Angelo*
*Lucca*
*Tel: 0583-47711*
Closed Sunday evening and Mon-

day. In business since 1414. Excellent Lucchese cuisine in gentrified rustic setting.

**VIPORE**
*Pieve di Santo Stefano – Lucca*
*Tel: 0583-394065*
Closed all day Monday and Tuesday lunch. Seasoned specialities in hilltop farmhouse.

**LA MORA**
*Ponte a Moriano*
*5 miles (9 km) from Lucca*
*Tel: 0583-406402*
Ravioli or roast lamb in an old post house.

**RISTORANTE CASALI**
*Via Marconi 6*
*Barga*
*Tel: 0583-723972*
Closed Tuesday.
In the summer you can eat on the terrace. Garfagnana cuisine.

**RISTORANTE CARLINO**
*Via Garibaldi 15*
*Castelnuovo di Garfagnana*
Closed Monday. Sample goat and pasta on the terrace.

**DA PROSPERO**
*Via Santa Lucia*
*Lucca*

**TADDEUCCI**
*Piazza San Michele*
*Lucca*
Good pastries. Try the *Pan Buccellato,* a round aniseed cake from Lucca.

**VINCENZO GUIDOTTI**
*Via di Piaggiori 119*
*Segromigno – near Lucca*
Honey and fruit preserved in honey.

**LIDO RICCI**
*Buetta di Pieve di Santo Stefano*
*Lucca*
Locally produced olive oil.

**IL CASTELLO**
*Via di Mezzo*
*Barga*
Antiques.

**MARCHETTI RENZO**
*Via di Mezzo*
*Barga*
Local sausage and cheese.

**IL GIGLIO GUELFO**
*Via del Pretorio*
*Barga*
Ceramics.

**CAMPOSANTO MONUMENTALE**
*Piazza Duomo*
*Pisa*
Ceramics.

**FELTRINELLI**
*Corso Italia 117*
*Pisa*
This is the best bookshop in town – includes good choice of books in English.

## Museums and Sights

Pisa has notoriously unreliable opening times, so it is best to double-check locally.

**MUSEO DELLE SINOPIE**
*Piazza Duomo*
*Pisa*
9.30am–12.40pm, 3–6.40pm.

**MUSEO DELL'OPERA DEL DUOMO**
*Piazza Duomo*
*Pisa*
9am–1pm, 3–5pm and later in summer.

**MUSEO NAZIONALE DI SAN MATTEO**
*Lungarno Mediceo,*
*Piazza San Matteo in Soarta*
*Pisa*
9am–7pm; Sunday and holidays 9am–1pm. Closed Monday.

**MUSEO NATIONALE DI VILLA GUINIGI**
*Via della Quaranoia*
*Lucca*
9am–2pm; holidays 9am–1pm; closed Monday.

**PINACOTECA NAZIONALE**
*Via Galli Tassi 43*
*Lucca*
9am–2pm; holidays 9am–1pm; closed Monday.

**GROTTA DEL VENTO**
*Fornovalasco – near Lucca*
*Tel: 0583-722024*
1 April to 31 October, 10am–noon, 3–6pm. Various tours available, which are best arranged in advance.

**PARCO DELLE ALPI APUANE**
*Castelnuovo di Garfagnana*
*Tel: 0583-644354*
Vast area. After hiking in the chestnut forests on a hill between Castelnuovo and Pieve Fosciana, you can buy mushrooms, honey and chestnuts.

**PARCO NATURALE ORECCHIELLA**
*Garfagnana*
Phone: 0583-619098
Interesting flora and fauna!

## Special Events

**Pisa**
**MAY** and **JUNE**: Concerts.
**JUNE 17:** *Luminara,* the previous day, when all the palazzi along the Lungarno are illuminated. The next day: the regatta.
**26 JUNE:** *Gioco del Ponte,* a medieval tug-of-war.

**Lucca**
**JULY** and **SEPTEMBER:** *Palio della Balestra,* crossbow shooting.
**SEPTEMBER:** *Settembre Lucchese Luminaria di Santa Croce:* religious procession.
*Mercato Antiquario:* every third weekend. Antiques fair.

**Torre del Lago Puccini**
**AUGUST:** Puccini festival.

**Anchiano (Borgo a Mozzano)**
**30 APRIL TO 1 MAY:** *Sagra del Baccala,* dried cod feast.

## Val d'Orcia

**To Monteriggioni and Siena; to the monastery of Monte Oliveto Maggiore and via Montalcino – where the famous Brunello is produced – up onto Monte Amiata; to Bagno Vignoni for a swim and via San Quirico to Pienza and Montepulciano. Allow two full days.**

From Florence you reach **Monteriggioni** via the *superstrada* to Siena; suddenly you will see the village, encircled by walls, as if straight out of a fresco by Simone Martini or Paolo Uccello. After a short walk we head on via the N2 to **Siena**.

Elsewhere in Tuscany there may be higher towers, richer museums – but the special thing about this city is that everything fits together. Siena shines in medieval perfection. In fact, as far back as the 13th century the builders endeavoured to conceive a whole into which the parts would fit harmoniously. Relations between Florence and Siena were never good: in 1230 the Florentines, witty as ever, catapulted excrement and donkey corpses over Siena's walls in the hope that their dear neighbours would die of the plague (a sort of forerunner of today's biological warfare).

Let's first look around the **Piazza del Campo**, a square in the shape of an amphitheatre. The cobblestones divide the Piazza into nine segments – meant to represent the *Governo dei Nove* ('Council

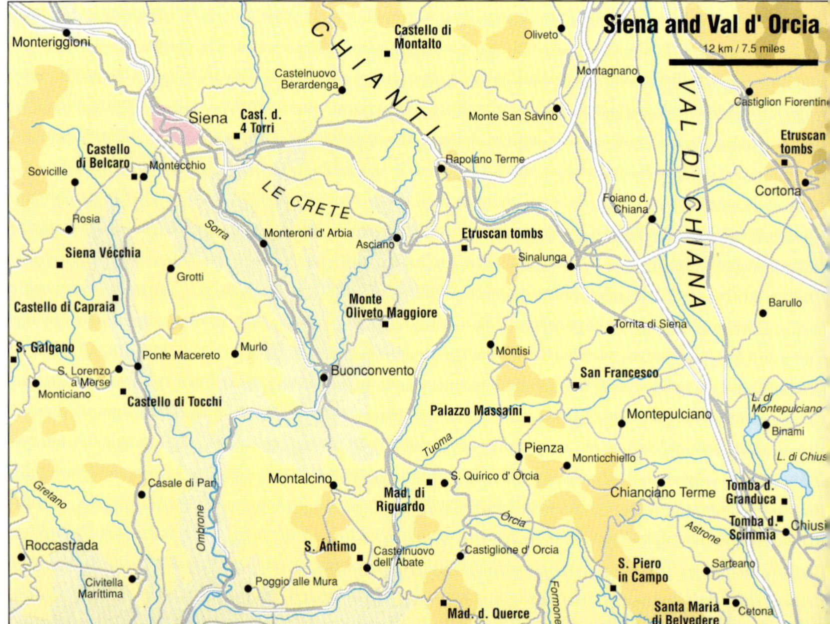

*View of Siena*

of the Nine'), who ruled the medieval city until the end of its golden age in 1355. In the centre of the upper part we have the **Fonte Gaia** fountain, a popular pigeon hangout. The **Palazzo Pubblico** is considered one of the most beautiful Gothic buildings in Tuscany. Its **Museo Civico**, more a fabulously decorated palace than a classic museum. The main council chamber is adorned with a Simone Martini Virgin and the celebrated fresco of a condottiere.

Who will join me in climbing to the top of the **Torre del Mangia**? From that height there is a glorious view of the Piazza and the rooftops. You will find the statue of the Mangia, the gluttonous bellringer, in the **Cortile del Podestà**. The **Cappella in Piazza** was erected in 1378 in thanksgiving for the end of the plague. The streets Via Banchi di Sotto, Via Banchi di Sopra and Via di Città divide Siena into three parts. Via di Città features the **Loggia della Mercanzia**, a temple of commerce, and the **Palazzo Chigi-Saracini** (seat of the Accademia Musicale Chigiana). Turning right onto Via del Capitano we see the Palazzo del Capitano di Giustizia.

The **Cathedral** – part Romanesque, part Gothic, because construction took so long – is perched on one of the three hills of Siena. Inside there is a pulpit by Nicola Pisano. To the left we come upon the **Libreria Piccolomini** (we will be coming across this name frequently during the course of this tour)

*Siena Cathedral*

*Palio in Siena*

housing the excellent illuminated codexes of Pope Pius II. The frescoes by Pinturicchio (1509) are not bad either. Other sights are: the Museo dell'Opera Metropolitana and the Pinacoteca Nazionale ('National Picture Gallery'); and the churches of San Domenico and San Francesco (frescoes by the Lorenzetti brothers).

It is difficult, I know, to say goodbye to Siena. But there is more that we want to see. Taking the N2 again – known as 'Via Cassia' to the Romans – drive for 16km (10 miles) to **Buonconvento**. Here we turn left onto the N451 and continue for another 9km (5½ miles) to the monastery of **Monte Oliveto Maggiore** (summer hours: 9am–12.30pm, 3–7pm; winter: 9am–12.30pm, 3–5.30pm; otherwise ring the bell). As you approach, you will already be able to see the brick-red cloister buildings glowing from afar among the green cypresses and olive trees. Founded by hermits in 1313, the abbey is still inhabited by monks – so it is a place of reflection and silence. The **Chiostro Grande** is particularly interesting with its frescoes portraying the life of St Benedict. The monks here still live as they did in the 14th century and produce their own wine, olive oil, honey and herbal liqueur.

We backtrack the 9km (6 miles) to the N2 (via Cassia) and drive another 3km (2 miles) to where the N323 branches off to **Montalcino**, a quiet town known for the delicacy of its wine. As so often in this country the landscape is simply beautiful. The fortress

*(Rocca)* is a reminder of the fact that Montalcino often fought on the side of Siena against Florence. On your way back down from the fortress you will pass an *enoteca* (wine shop) where you can try the exquisite Brunello (full-bodied red wine) along with the familiar *crostini*. On Piazza del Popolo look for the austere **Palazzo Comunale**, on Piazza Garibaldi the **Sant'Agostino** church.

Five kilometres (3 miles) from Montalcino you can stop at the **Fattoria dei Barbi** to sample the wine in the *cantina* – perhaps buying a bottle or two for later – and have something to eat in the *taverna*. Another 5km (3 miles) down the road we come upon the Romanesque abbey of **Sant'Antimo**, built in the 12th century on the ruins of a 9th-century church said to have been founded by Charlemagne.

It is a further 5km (3 miles) to **Monte Amiata**, a popular skiing area and another mile to a turn-off on the left to **Bagno Vignoni**. This little town is most evocative in the winter, when darkness is falling. We park. Then as we turn the corner, we are suddenly enveloped by steam. The yellowish light of the lanterns dimly illuminates the stone façades of the buildings lining the square. The vapours grow denser the harder we peer and suddenly the square turns out to be a huge basin full of bubbling sulfurous water. Before it was forbidden we used to swim here in the darkness of night, drinking sparkling wine. Now you have to go to the **Posta Marcucci** (Phone: 0577-887112) which pumps the water from this historical pool – where even Lorenzo de'Medici and Saint Catharine bathed – into its own private swimming pools.

On the Piazza with the pool you also have the **Hotel Le Terme** (tel: 0577-887150), which is said to have been built by Rossellino, the municipal master builder of Pienza. Both Bagno Vignoni and S Galgano were well-kept secrets until Tarkovsky, the Russian filmmaker, used them as backdrops for scenes in his film *Nostalgia*. The remains of the medieval village of

**Vignone** (10 houses, as well as a small Romanesque church, a well and lots of cats) are nearby (8km/5 miles).

After driving another 6km (4 miles) along the N2 (Via Cassia), we turn left to **S Quírico d'Orcia**, both historically and economically the 'capital' of the Val d'Orcia because of its location on the road built by the Lombards in the 7th century leading from France to

Rome. In medieval times the traders and pilgrims using this route filled the hospices and monasteries in S Quirico, contributing to its development.

The masterpiece of S Quirico is a Romanesque church built on the ruins of a presbytery going back to the 8th century. The three terrible monsters on the architrave hardly contributed to dispelling the darkness of the Middle Ages. The 16th-century grounds of **Orti Leonini** are also worth seeing.

Ten kilometres (6 miles) further down the N146 we reach **Pienza**, the utopia developed by the humanist, poet and later Pope, Silvio Piccolomini. On the way to Pienza we come to **Pieve di Corsignano**, the 12th-century church where the little boy Enea Silvio, later to become Pope Pius II, was baptised. Here, too, note the demonic ornamentation. Here in the parish church of the former village of Corsignano is where Silvio conceived the idea of building a new town called the Pius-City of Pienza, according to Renaissance and humanist principles. The most significant buildings in Pienza – the **Cattedrale dell'Assunta** (1492), the **Palazzo Piccolomini** and the **Palazzo Pubblico** – are all on the atmospheric main square. In Pienza, by the way, you can buy excellent *pecorino* (cheese).

The road then winds upwards for 12km (7½ miles) to another small Renaissance town, one of the few hardly affected by tourism:

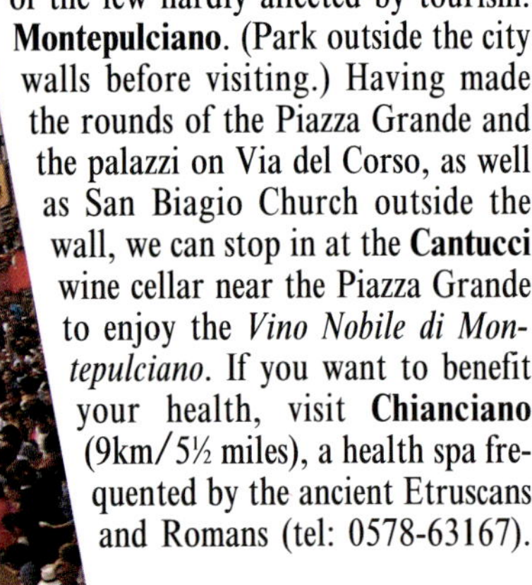

**Montepulciano**. (Park outside the city walls before visiting.) Having made the rounds of the Piazza Grande and the palazzi on Via del Corso, as well as San Biagio Church outside the wall, we can stop in at the **Cantucci** wine cellar near the Piazza Grande to enjoy the *Vino Nobile di Montepulciano*. If you want to benefit your health, visit **Chianciano** (9km/5½ miles), a health spa frequented by the ancient Etruscans and Romans (tel: 0578-63167).

## Hotels

**CERTOSA DI MAGGIANO**
*Strada di Certosa 82*
*Siena*
*Tel: 0577-288180*
Double: 460,000 lire
The oldest Carthusian monastery
in Tuscany with frescoes and an-
tiques. Swimming pool, tennis
court and park. De-luxe

**TRE DONZELLE**
*Via delle Donzelle 5*
*Siena*
*Tel: 0577-280358*
Double: 55,000 lire
Centrally located.

**CASA DEL PELLEGRINO**
*Via Camporeggio 31*
*Siena*
*Tel: 0577-44177*
Double: 50,000 lire
Rooms with views.

**IL MARZOCCO**
*Piazza Savonarola*
*Montepulciano*
*Tel: 0578-757262*
Double: 90,000 lire
Medieval palazzo.

**ALBERGO POSTA MARCUCCI**
*Bagno Vignoni*
*Tel: 0577-887112*
Double: 150,000 lire
Half-board; swimming pool.

**LE TERME**
*Via delle Sorgenti 13*
*Bagno Vignoni*
*Tel: 0577-887150*
Double: 68,000 lire
Atmosphere of days gone by.

**ROCCOLO DI PALAZZUOLO**
*Palazzuolo – San Quirico*
*d'Orcia*
*Tel: 0577-897080*
Double: 90,000 lire
In lush countryside with terrace.
Tuscan cuisine.

**HOTEL CORSIGNANO**
*Via della Madonnina 11*
*Pienza*
*Tel: 0587-748501*
Double: 105,000 lire
Renovated; near the Duomo.

**IL CHIOSTRO DI PIENZA**
*Corso Rosellino 26*
*Pienza*
Double: 140,000 lire
Tel: 0578-0748400
Former medieval monastery.

## Restaurants

You can eat well and not too expensively throughout the Val d'Orcia. The regional specialities are: *pici,* a special pasta dish, hare and wild pork in sweet and sour sauce, *pecorino* and *soprassata* (pork sausages).

### RISTORANTE IL POZZO
*Piazza Roma 2*
*Monteriggioni – near Siena*
*Tel: 0577-304127*
Closed Sunday and Monday. Come here for rustic specialities such as stuffed pigeon, mushrooms, rabbit, homemade pasta and apple pie.

### OSTERIA LE LOGGE
*Via del Porrione 33*
*Siena*
*Tel: 0577-48013*
Closed Sunday. Atmospheric building with 19th-century interior. Specialises in typical Sienese cuisine. Popular, so either book or arrive early.

### RISTORANTE TURIDDU
*Via Stalloreggi 62*
*Siena*
*Tel: 0577-282121*
Closed Sunday evening and Monday. Restorante Turiddu is a popular choice among locals. Inexpensive.

### LA TORRE
*Via di Salicotti 7–9*
*Siena*
*Tel: 0577-287548*
Closed Thursday.
Popular with the locals, inexpensive.

### MEDIO EVO
*Via dei Rossi 40*
*Siena*
*Tel: 0577-290315*
Closed Thursday. Charmingly set in medieval palazzo. Moderate prices.

### GELATERIA FONTE GAIA
*Piazza del Campo*
*Siena*
First-class ice cream.

### VECCHIO FORNO
*Via Piazzola 8*
*S.Quirico D'Orcia*
*Tel: 0577-897380*
For between-meal snacks.

### DA FALCO
*Piazza Dante 7*
*Pienza*
*Tel: 0578-748551*
Closed Friday. Simple Tuscan cuisine at low prices. Also small, fairly basic hotel.

### IL PRATO
*Piazza Dante Alighieri 25*
*Pienza*
*Tel: 0578-748601*
Closed Wednesday. Home-made *pici* (thick spaghetti), roast meats and pecorino cheese in beamed room.

### POGGIO ANTICO
*Poggio Antico/Montalcino*
*Tel: 0577-849200*
Top Tuscan restaurant in lovely rural setting.

**Taverna della Fattoria dei Barbi**
*Montalcino/Località Podernovi*
*Tel: 0577-849357*
Open 12.30pm–12.30am, closed Tuesday and Wednesday. Wine-growing estate which also sells ham and salami.

**La Cucina di Edgardo**
*Via Saloni 9*
*Montalcino*
*Tel: 0577-848232*
Closed Wednesday. In the old town. *Cucina nuova*, very chic. Reservations required.

## Museums and Sights

**Museo Civico**
*Piazza del Campo 1*
*Siena*
9.30am–7.45pm; Sunday, holidays and winter: 9.30am–1pm.

**Museo dell'Opera Metropolitana**
*Piazza del Duomo 8*
*Siena*
Summer: 9am–7.30pm; winter: 9am–1.30pm.

**Pinacoteca Nazionale**
*Via San Pietro 29*
*Siena*
8.30am–7pm; Sunday 8.30am–1pm; closed pm in winter; closed Monday.

**Pinacoteca Crociani e Museo Civico**
*Via Ricci 15*
*Montepulciano*
9.20am–1pm; closed Monday.

**Palazzo Piccolomini**
*Piazza Pio II*
*Pienza*
10am–12.30pm, 3–6pm; closed Monday.

**Le Terme**
*Via Dante 35*
*Bagno Vignoni*
*Tel: 0577-887150*
15th-century palazzo beside medieval thermal baths.

## Special Events

**Siena**
**July-August:** *Settimane Musicali Senesi*
**July:** Jazz Festival
**2 July** and **16 August:** *Palio,* the celebrated horse race.

**Montalcino**
**Middle of July:** *Festival del Teatro* held outdoors.

**Montepulciano**
**Last Sunday in August:** Barrel race.

## Elba

**You should visit at least one of the islands of the Tuscan archipelago: Elba is the largest and has the most varied landscape. Once around the island and then a swim in a beautiful cove.**

Nearly 30km (20 miles) long and 20km (12 miles) wide, and with 150km (94 miles) of coastline, Elba is the largest of the islands in the Tuscan archipelago. With its turquoise-coloured waters and numerous beaches and coves, it is no wonder that the island attracts millions of tourists every year. August is the worst possible time to visit this island; June and September are probably the best months, but spring begins here as early as March, when the *macchia* is in bloom. Allow at least a day to drive around the island. If staying overnight, book accommodation in advance if possible (*see page 91*). You can reach Elba by train from Pisa to Piombino (Via Campiglia Marittima) and from the port catch a ferry or hydrofoil to Portoferráio, the Elban capital. The crossing takes between 30 minutes and an hour. Consider hiring a car in Portoferráio (Maggiore, tel: 915 386) or enquire about tours from the tourist office (Calata Italia 26; tel: 0565-914671).

Elba's first inhabitants were the Etruscans, who grew wealthy here quarrying the minerals. In the course of their history the

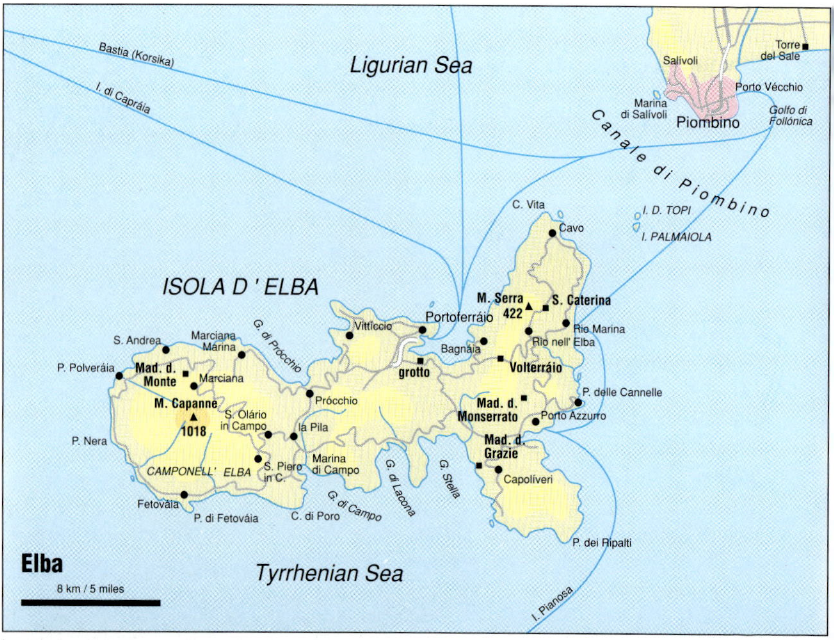

*The impressive coast*

Elbans have often had to fend off attacking pirates. *The* big event in the history of the island, however, was Napoleon's ten-month exile on Elba (see the **Villa dei Mulini** in Portoferraio and **Villa S Martino**, 6km (4 miles) from Portoferraio).

Geographically the island can be devided into three sections: the western, undeveloped part consists of a granite massif with Monte Capanne rising to an elevation of 1,021m/3,350ft – with an impressive view of almost the entire island. The west offers good hiking through lovely landscapes with alternating chestnut woods and *macchia* thickets. The coast is rocky and the coves are small but they make up for this by being much less crowded than in other areas. The middle section is more reminiscent of the Tuscan mainland, with olive groves, vineyards and fruit plantations.

The east is known for its deposits of iron ore and other minerals, which are still being mined today. The earth here displays a full range of shades. In addition to the cultivated plants widespread on the mainland, such as olive trees, cypresses and pines, there are also cork oaks, eucalyptus trees, agaves and palms. The *macchia* blossoms in more glorious colours than on the mainland. The sea is full of fish, much to the delight of divers and anglers. The underwater landscape is dominated by sponges and corals.

**Portoferráio**, our port of arrival, is an unusual place: despite the masses of tourists here year in, year out, it has nevertheless managed to preserve its original way of life. A third of the inhabitants of the island live here: in all around 12,000 people.

*Fortress on Elba*

Assuming you have not already had your fill of churches, castles, fortresses and abbeys, you can help yourself to an extra ration here on Elba. For proof that there is plenty to see here, try the walk into the old town: from Piazza della Repubblica to Darsena, including the **Porta a Mare**, and then on to the **Torre della Linguinella**. For more lively impressions visit the **Galeazze Market** (Piazza Cavour), where everything that the island and its waters bring forth is for sale; or check out Piazza della Repubblica any Friday afternoon.

From Portoferraio we drive to **Rio nell'Elba**, a former fortress built for defence against attacking pirates. Situated high up on a rock, it is one of the oldest settlements on the island (a 10km/6 mile detour to **Cavo** will take you through a rather lonely landscape). **Rio Marina** (Palazzo Comunale, Collezione Ricci and Mineral Collection), the harbour of Rio nell'Elba, has a number of good restaurants. Next we head for **Porto Azzurro**, the island's second-largest harbour with two fortresses, Forte Longone and Forte Focardo; one of them being an infamous prison from which a well-known right-wing extremist attempted an escape, ensuring that all of Italy held its breath for several days. Further up you will find the pretty village of **Capoliveri.** Located south of Capoliveri, the **Fattoria Ripalte** rents out rooms, apartments and entire villas. The peninsula belonging to the Fattoria is at the disposal of the hotel guests. This is one of the best addresses for an extended stay on Elba – provided that you are reasonably well-off.

Passing the touristic towns of **Lacona**, (large pretty beach: Spiaggia Grande) and **Marina di Campo** (unbearable in midsummer), we reach **Cávoli** and **Fetováia** where there are good beaches. **Punta delle Tombe**, however, is less populated. From here we enter the 'Wild West'. If you can do without nightlife, you will have a good time on this coastline, stretching from **Pomonte** to **S Andrea** (the view from Sedia di Napoleone is superb). For children the area is less suitable because of the lack of sandy beaches. From **Colle d'Orano** there is a path leading down to the somewhat stony but empty beach. **Cala della Cotaccia** is a comfortable cove with large, flat rocks. Behind **Capo S Andrea**, where the hotels are all rather ugly, there are several quiet guest-houses among shady trees. The **Pensione Oleandro** (tel: 0565-908088) also has a good restaurant with a terrace directly above the sea.

The road then makes its way up through chestnut woods to **Marciana Alta**, the oldest settlement on Elba. The beautiful church of **Madonna del Monte** can be reached on foot and a cable car goes to the top of **Monte Capanne** (otherwise take the footpath Sentiero N1 – distance: 5km (3 miles), difference in elevation: 375m (1,230ft); two hours and 40 minutes from the steps under the Mediciesque gate next to S Lorenzo Church). **Poggio** is a small mountain village with narrow alleyways, known for its mineral water springs.

Back at the bottom we can visit **Marciana Marina**, a tiny harbour town (visit the Piazza Vittorio Emanuele) which is becoming more and more popular. Next we have the large bays of **Procchio** and **Biódola** (classy: Hotel Hermitage, tel: 0565-936911). From here there are two interesting detours: to **Capo d'Enfola** (including hiking trails) and to the small, pretty village of **Vitíccio**.

Arriving back in Portoferraio it's time to make a decision: to cross back to the mainland or to jump on a ferry heading for the small volcanic island of **Capraia** 20km (12½ miles) away – complete with goats and a crater lake!

## Practical Information
### Hotels

**ASSOCIAZIONE ALBERGATORI**
*Calata Italia 21*
*Portoferraio*
*Tel: 0565-914754*
Phone or visit to make reservations at hotels in the region. In summer you may be obliged to accept half or full board.

**'APE ELBANA**
*Via Cosimo dei Medici 1*
*Portoferraio*
*Tel: 0565-914245*
Double: 80,000 lire.

**FABRICIA**
*Località Magazzini,*
*Portoferraio*
*Tel: 0565-933181*
Full-board: 500,000 lire for two. Stylish, modern, luxury complex set in an olive grove

**PENSIONE OLEANDRO**
*Cottoncello – S Andrea*
*Tel: 0565-908088*
Double: 70,000 lire

**HOTEL DA GIACOMINO**
*Capo S. Andrea*
*Tel: 0565-908010*
Double: 58,000–100,000 lire. Offers pool, solarium, panoramic views. Full-board: 250,000 lire for two.

*Fortress and sea*

### Bel Tramonto
*Località Patresi*
*Marciana*
*Tel: 0565-908027*
Small hotel with lovely grounds.
Double: 150,000 lire.

### La Acacie
*Località Narengo*
*Capoliveri*
*Tel: 0565-935151*
Mediterranean-style complex.
Half-board: 300,000 lire for two.

## Restaurants

### Le Ghiaie
*Piazza del Popolo*
*Portoferraio*
*Tel: 0565-914276*
Closed Monday.

### Trattoria da Lido
*Salità di Falcone 2*
*Portoferraio*
*Tel: 0565-914650*

### Olga
*Via dell'Amore 54*
*Portoferraio*
*Tel: 0565-917446*
Inspired Lovorno-style cuisine.

### Publius
*Piazza XX Settembre*
*Località Poggio, Marciana*
*Tel: 0565-99208*
Three km from Marciana. Fine views, Elban wines and fish dishes as well as game. pricey.

### Ristorante Il Chiasso
*Vicolo N. Sauroa*
*Capoliveri*
*Tel: 0565-968709*
Closed Tuesday. Menu includes risotto with cuttlefish, sole stuffed with shrimps.

## Special Events

**17 January:** S Antonio: *Capoliveri* – when horses and riders are blessed.

**Sunday prior to Shrove Tuesday:** Carnival in Porto Azzurro, a fashionable port.

**1 May:** Portoferraio: Parade in historic costumes in honour of Napoleon.

**1st week in July:** Elba Jazz festival.

## The Casentino and Arezzo

**From Florence to the ruins of Romena Castle and Stia; the Hermitage of Camaldoli; by way of Poppi and Bibbiena to the monastery at La Verna; to Caprese, the birthplace of Michelangelo; on to Arezzo (Piero della Francesca country) and Cortona. Allow at least a day to explore this charming border of Tuscany and Umbria, ideally with an overnight stop in Arezzo or Cortona.**

The name **Casentino** refers to the upper Arno Valley, an area isolated from the rest of the world and as yet almost totally undiscovered by non-Italian tourism. From our starting point in Florence we drive to **Pontassieve** and then take the N70 over the **Consuma Pass** in the direction of Poppi, but 20km (12½ miles) past Consuma we turn off to the left to **Romena Castle.** Dante was once given lodgings here. The nearby Romanesque church of **S Pieve di Romena** is also interesting. Our next stop is **Stia** with its **Castello di Porciano.** We then take the N310 until we come to a road on the left leading off to the Hermitage (*Eremo*) of **Camáldoli** with its picturesque but gloomy location in a ravine. Founded in the 11th century, the monastery is still inhabited but the monks also run a welcoming café here. The old cloister pharmacy with its mortars and crucibles is a pleasing relic of past times.

Unless you decide to stay and join the 'hermits' you should press on via **Moggiona** and **Pratale** to **Poppi** with its majestic castle. A tour through the narrow streets, with their arcades and steep steps, is impressive because of the silent and dreamy atmosphere.

Continuing on the N70 takes us to **Bibbiena**, mainly known for its salami. Then we turn left onto the N208 to reach **La Verna** (14th century ), a busy place of pilgrimage – it was here that St Francis of Assisi received the stigmata in 1224. From here it is another 15km (9

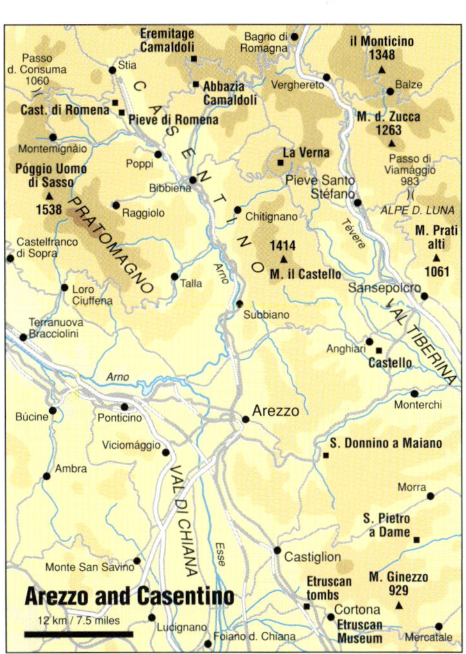

*Arezzo*

miles) to **Caprese Michelangelo**, where it is possible to tour the secluded house where the artist was born. We backtrack to **Chiusi della Verna**, then head on via **Chitignano** to the N71 and **Arezzo**.

Personalities such as Petrarch, Pietro Aretino and Vasari were born here – but they all left the city sooner or later. Only Piero della Francesca (1410–92) remained long enough to provide Arezzo with its great attraction: the frescoes in the S **Francesco** church. The churches of S Domenico and S Maria della Pieve are worth a visit, as is the house in which Giorgio Vasari was born. On the **Piazza Grande** we can admire some magnificent palazzi. On the first Sunday in September this is the site of the annual medieval tournament or joust, the *Giostra del Saracino.* On the first Sunday of each month the *Fiera Antiquaria* is held here, when antique dealers, private collectors and bargain-hunters haggle.

The next stage of our journey is full of beautiful scenery: from Arezzo via Palazzo di Pero to **Castiglion Fiorentino** with its mediaeval circular wall. Just outside we come across the strange octagonal church of S **Maria della Consolazione**. Another six miles (10km) on and we reach **Cortona** which already has quite an Umbrian air to it. Even upon arrival one cannot overlook its dominant fortress. On a clear day one has a fabulous view from **Piazza Garibaldi**, at the entrance to the old town, all the way to the Lake Trasimeno. On Piazza della Repubblica, the centre of activity, the principal buildings are the Palazzo Comunale and the Palazzo Casali.

Let us make one final detour, taking us 2km (1¼ miles) outside Cortona in the direction of Camucia, to the Renaissance church of **Madonna del Calcinaio.** On 14–15 August the *Sagra della Bistecca*, a huge steak blow-out, is held in Cortona. The city is full of barbecues and an unmistakable *bistecca* aroma; by the end of the night entire rivers of red wine have been guzzled.

If I may, to bring this to a happy conclusion, I would like to

venture a suggestion which I am not really authorised to make —
since it does not lie within the bounds of Tuscany: the perfect finale
would be a detour to **Lake Trasimeno**, taking the ferry to **Isola
del Trasimeno** (lodging at Hotel Sauro).

## Practical Information
### Hotels

**GRAND HOTEL MINERVA**
*Via Fiorentina 4*
*Arezzo*
*Tel: 0575-370390*
Double: 130,000 lire.

**CONTINENTALE**
*Piazza Guido Monaco 7*
*Arezzo*
*Tel: 0575-20251*
Double: 130,000 lire

**SAN MICHELE**
*Via Guelfa 15*
*Cortona*
*Tel: 0575-604348*
Delightfully restored Renaissance
palazzo set in the historic centre.

**CASTELLO DI GARGONZA**
*Gargonza, Monte San Savino*
*15 miles (25km) from Arezzo*
*Tel: 0575-847021*
Double: 200,000 lire. A restored
medieval village with B&B or
self-catering facilities and traditional restaurant.

## Restaurants

**RISTORANTE LE TASTEVIN**
*Via de'Cenci 9*
*Arezzo*
*Tel: 0575-28304*
Closed Monday. Tuscan dishes.
Also pizzeria and piano bar.

**LA BUCA DI SAN FRANCESCO**
*Via S.Francesco 1*
*Closed Monday and Tuesday.*
Rustic  cellar restaurant near S
Francesco church. Trecento fres-
coes and Tuscan dishes.

**LOGGETTA**
*Piazza Pescheria 3*
*Cortona*
*Tel: 0575-630575*
Tuscan dishes in a stylish setting:
the converted wine cellars of a
Renaissance palace.

**ANTICA TRATTORIA PRINCIPE**
*Via Giovi 25, Giovi*
*Tel: 0575-362046*
Closed Monday.
Rustic, charmingly old-fashioned
8km (5 miles) from Arezzo.

# Eating Out

*Quant'è bella giovinezza*

*che si fugge tuttavia*
*Chi vuol esser lieto si*
*Di doman non c'è certezza.*

*Blissful youth with neither pain nor*
  *sorrow*
*soon will be mouldering in the ground*
*where no more merriment will be found*
*No one is certain about tomorrow.*

**Lorenzo il Magnifico**

In Florence, you can eat well, for sure – but cheap is another story. Tuscan cuisine involves some of the best and healthiest cooking in Italy, although the selection of dishes is no longer as large as it used to be. It is an old and prudent school of cooking based on the preparation of spicy and tasty ingredients in an uncomplicated manner – thus their digestibility. This simplicity is more apparent than actual, for the success of this 'plain' style of cooking depends on proportion and balance and relies highly on the eye and nose. What is simpler than slapping a piece of meat on the grill, but who is actually able to prepare a true *bistecca alla fiorentina*? Even the Etruscans (as we discover on some of the frescoes) made fresh pasta and grilled chicken and other meats in the way they are prepared throughout Tuscany today. By the municipal era, Tuscan cuisine was more or less established. During the period of the Signoria, when Florence's trade relationships and banking activities had made it one of the most important centres of Europe, refined dining played an important role in Florentine commerce and culture. As early as the 14th century, at least a hundred years before the rest of Europe, Tuscans were dining with

forks. Thanks to the nation-
ality and home ports of the
discoverers of the Americas,
certain spices, tomatoes and
especially beans – all of
these being basic ingredients for plain cooking –
were introduced to Tus-
cany. Indeed, the Floren-
tines are often dubbed 'Mangiafagioli'

('bean-eaters') by other Italians. Through the chefs
of the royal household of Caterina de'Medici, the wife of Henry II
– and later through the influence of Maria de'Medici who married
Henry IV in 1600 – Tuscan cuisine even influenced the exquisite
French cuisine: these gourmet queens, in fact, exported such delicacies
as *canard à l'orange* and *soup à l'oignon* to France.

## Typical Tuscan dishes

The most noteworthy appetizers are *crostini* (small slices of white
bread spread with a sort of warm liver paste) and *affettati misti*, ie
*prosciutto* (the Tuscan ham is saltier than the better-known Parma
ham), *salame* (pork sausage with coarse pieces of fat and whole
peppercorns), *finocchiona* (a softer type of sausage with fennel) and
*soprassata* (another type of soft, fresh sausage). As *primi* (first courses)
soups are more traditional than pasta dishes. These include *panzanella*
or bread soups, a cold, refreshing summer dish, and *pappa al pomodoro*,
and *ribollita*, the heavier winter dishes.

The pasta dish I particularly recommend is the delicious *pappardelle
alla lepre* (fresh egg noodle strips with hare ragout). Simple but
popular peasant dishes are *pasta e fagioli* (short pasta with beans,
olive oil and sage) or *pasta e ceci* (pasta with chickpeas). For gourmets
there are also *gnocchi* (small cornmeal dumplings) or *crespelle* (thin
crêpes with various fillings), especially exquisite with *ricotta* (a mild
sort of curd cheese) and spinach.

Moving on to the *secondi* (main courses): in Tuscany meat has
priority over fish, and game is rightfully held in special esteem. In
the Maremma they eat wild pork and hare; in other regions they
favour quail and thrush. When it comes to pork the preferred fare
is *arista* (from the Greek word *aristos*, the best): a piece of loin
spiked with rosemary and garlic and slowly roasted. Or *salsicce*,
pork sausages: some love them raw, spread on bread, others fried
and with beans. Pork liver is wrapped in a net of fat, decorated
with bay leaves, skewered and roasted. Chicken and rabbit are preferred deep fried, served with french-fried zucchini florets or artichokes
on the side. We must not forget *trippa alla fiorentina*: tripe in tomato
sauce. It is not dog food – I swear!

Fish enthusiasts will not want to miss the *cacciucco* in Livorno:
get it while it is hot, because it is hot! Compared with this local
concoction, *bouillabaise* is simply plain old fish soup. It is quite

rough going for vegetarians in Tuscany: white beans, asparagus with egg, artichokes in *pinzimonio* (raw and dipped into olive oil leaf by leaf) – that just about sums it up. Of course, every restaurant serves the ubiquitous *insalata mista*, but that is about as Tuscan as Welsh rarebit. Our cheese *par excellence,* on the other hand, is *pecorino* – a sheep's cheese which is made by Sardinian shepherds. In Tuscany shepherding is, alas, a dying profession.

Tuscan desserts are the *castagnaccio* (chestnut meal, pinenuts, nuts, raisins, rosemary, salt and olive oil), *schiacciata con l'uva* (puff pastry with black grapes), the plain *schiacciata alla fiorentina,* or *cenci* (literally: 'rags' or 'cloths', due to their tattered appearance). *Biscotti di Prato* (with almonds and dunked in *vinsanto*) can only be recommended to people with no dental problems! In Siena one should definitely try the medieval *panforte di Siena*: one cubic millimetre has more calories than an entire chocolate cake. *Zuppa inglese* (trifle) is no more English than florentines are from Florence, or hamburgers are from Hamburg.

Well, do I dare to even begin on the subject of wines – with the vast variety available here? All right, then; white wines: *Vernaccia di San Gimignano, Montecarlo, Bianco di Pitigliano, Pomino, Bolgheri* and, for everyday drinking, *Galestro*. As far as red wines are concerned, this task is more difficult. In addition to the various Chianti Classico wines which are practically all good, there are the non-classical types of chianti: *chianti dei colli aretini, dei colli fiorentini, colli senesi, solline pisane,* etc, depending on the specific geographical location from which the grapes originate.

Red wines worth singling out for special attention are: *Montescudaio, Carmignano* and *Pomino*. But the finest of all (and the heaviest) are the *Brunello di Montalcino* and the *Vino Nobile di Montepulciano*. The sweet wines include *Vinsanto* and *Morellino* from Elba. *Salute!*

## Restaurants in Florence
### International Cuisine:

**ACQUARELLO**
*Via Ghibellina 156r*
*Tel: 055-2340544*
Closed Thursday. Offers elegant atmosphere in old palazzo. A good option for after theatre dining or a special occasion.

**HARRY'S BAR**
*Lungarno Vespucci 22r*
*Tel: 055-2396700*
Closed Sunday. Harry's Bar is known for good quality international and American-Italian cuisine.

## AL LUME DI CANDELA
*Via delle Terme 23r*
*Tel: 055-29456*
Closed Sunday. Classic cuisine in a medieval tower.

## RISTORANTE CORSINI
*Lungarno Corsini 4*
*Tel: 055-217706*
Closed Wednesday. Elegant.

## DONEY
*Piazza Strozzi 18*
*Tel: 055-2398206*
Closed Sunday and Monday.

## TAVERNA DEL BRONZINO
*Via delle Ruote 25r*
*Tel: 055-495220*
Closed Sunday.
Good but pricey cuisine, noble Tuscan surroundings.

## GARGA
*Via del Moro 50–52r*
*Tel: 055-2398898*
Closed Sunday lunch and all day Monday. Currently very 'in'.

## DANNY ROCK
*Via Pandolfini 13*
*Tel: 055-2340307*
Closed Monday.
Excellent crêpes.

## Tuscan Cuisine

## CIBREO
*Via dei Macci 118r*
*Tel: 055-2341100*
Closed Sunday and Monday.
Haunt of celebrities; branch in Tokyo; very good 'modernised' Old Tuscan cooking in a pleasant environment. No pasta.

## BUCA LAPI
*Via del Trebbio*
*Tel: 055-213768*
Closed Sunday.
Typical cellar restaurant in the Antinori palazzo, walls papered with newspaper. Great steak.

## CANTINETTA ANTINORI
*Piazza Antinori 3*
*Tel: 055-292234*
Closed Saturday and Sunday.
Typical Tuscan cuisine and house wine in noble *palazzo* – elegant atmosphere. Quite pricey.

## DA NOI
*Via Fiesolana 46r*
*Tel: 055-242917*
Closed Sunday and Monday.
The ambience is really nothing special, but Da Noi offers some of the finest cooking in town. Expensive. Book.

**COCO LEZZONE**
*Via del Parioncino 26,*
*Tel: 055-287178*
Closed Tuesday evening, Sunday and August. Tuscan peasant fare, including *ribollita* (thick soup), but not peasant prices.

**SOSTANZA (DETTO IL TROIA)**
*Via del Porcellana 25r*
*Tel: 055-212691*
Closed Saturday and Sunday. The best *bistecca alla fiorentina*. Casual atmosphere. Moderate prices.

### Out of Town:

**CAFFE CONCERTO**
*Lungarno Cristoforo*
*Colombo 7*
*Tel: 055-677377*
Closed Sunday.
On the Arno; *nouvelle cuisine.*

**ALBERGACCIO SERRISTORI**
*Scopeti – S Casciano*
*Loc. S Andrea in Percussina*
*Tel: 055-828471*
Closed Monday.
Ideal destination for a trip outside the city. Plain cooking. Delightful wine. Rarely does anyone exit the place sober.

**ETRUSCA**
*Piazza Mino 2*
*Fiesole*
*Tel: 055-599484*
Closed Friday.

**S DOMENICO**
*Piazza S Domenico 11*
*Fiesole*
*Tel: 055-59182*
Closed Wednesday.

**LE CAVE DI MAIANO**
*Via delle Cave 16*
*Maiano – Fiesole*
*Tel: 055-59133*
Closed Thursday and Sunday evening. Rustic ambience. Popular in summer.

**OMERO**
*Via Pian dei Giullari 11r, Arcetri*
*Tel: 055-220053*
Closed Tuesday.
Good cuisine, game specialities; on a hill 5km/3 miles from town.

### Typical Trattorie

**ALLA VECCHIA BETTOLA**
*Viale L.Ariosto 32–34r*
*Tel: 055-224158*
Closed Sunday and Monday. Traditional Tuscan

**BORDINO**
*Via Stracciatella 9r*
*Tel: 055-213048*
Closed Sunday.
Conveniently located close by the
Ponte Vecchio.

**ALESSI**
*Via di Mezzo 26r*
*Tel: 055-241821*
Closed Sunday.
Excellent cuisine – also unusual
dishes and humane prices. The
catch: mile-long queues.

**BORGO ANTICO**
*Piazza S Spirito 6r*
*Tel: 055-210437*
Closed Monday.
In the summer you can eat out-
side on the beautiful Piazza.

**DA GANINO**
*Piazza dei Cimatori 4*
*Tel: 055-214125*
Closed Sunday.
For a bite at noon, between mu-
seum visits and shopping. Quite
close to the Duomo.

**IL CANTINONE**
*Via Santo Spirito 6r*
*Tel: 055-218898*
Closed Monday.
Rustic ambience, no com-
plete meals, plain Tuscan
cooking; large selection of
wines. Italians rarely come
in here – German and
American are the business
languages. Moderated
prices.

**LATINI**
*Via dei Palchetti 6*
*Tel: 055-210916*
Closed Monday. Latini
is set in the Palazzo Rucellai.
Very lively atmosphere. Unsuit-

able choice for a romantic *tête-
à-tète* by candlelight.

**MARIO**
*Via Rosina 2r*
*Tel: 055-218550*
Closed Sunday.
Opens at noon. Cheep and cheer-
ful option, but truly Tuscan.

**ANTICO FATTORE**
*Via Lambertesca 1*
*Tel: 055-2881215*
Closed Sunday and Monday.
Mountains of pasta; plus tripe
and tomatoes.

**DI' CAMBI**
*Via S.Onofrio 1r*
*Tel: 055-217134*
Closed Sunday.
In the characterful quarter of San
Frediano; authentic Florentine
cuisine. Inexpensive.

## Pizzerias

**EDY HOUSE**
*Piazza Savonarola 9r*
*Tel: 055-588886*
Closed Tuesday.

**I Tarocchi**
*Via dei Renai 14r*
*Tel: 055-2343912*
Closed Monday. Inexpensive option. An unsurpassed selection of *primi*.

## Fish

**Capannina di Sante**
*Piazza Ravenna*
*Tel: 055-688345*
Closed Sunday. Set on the banks of the Arno.

**Pierrot**
*Via Fra' Taddeo Gaddi 25r*
*Tel: 055-702100*
Closed Sunday. Always a warm welcome.

**Silvio**
*Via del Parione 74–76r*
*Tel: 055-214005*
Closed Sunday.

## Ethnic

Florentines are not very daring as far as their stomachs or palates are concerned. Their motto on this subject tends to be: 'Cobbler, stick to your last!'. However, here are a few ethnic restaurants worth trying.

## Chinese

**China Town**
*Via Vecchietti 6r*
*Tel: 055-294470*
Closed Tuesday.

**Il Mandarino**
*Via Condotta 17r*
*Tel: 055-2396130*
Closed Monday.

**Lago – Siu**
*Via Pisana 16r*
*Tel: 055-223145*
Closed Monday.

## Japanese

**Japanese Restaurant Etto**
*Via de' Neri 72r*
*Tel: 055-210940*
Closed Monday.

## Jewish

**Il Cuscussu**
*Via Farini 2a*
*Tel: 055-241890*
Closed in the evening on Friday, Saturday and Sunday. Next door to the synagogue.

## Vegetarian

**Sedano Allegro**
*Borgo La Croce 20r*
*Tel: 055-2345505*
Closed Monday.

## Wine Bars

Unfortunately, wine bars, an old Florentine institution, are becoming fewer and fewer. They are, however, great places for a bite to eat, often serving everything from *panino* to complete meals.

**Angiolino**
*Via dell'Agnolo 107r*
Closed Sunday.

**Antica Mescita S. Niccolo**
*Via S.Niccolo' 60-62r*
Closed Sunday.

**Da Za Za**
*Piazza del Mercato Centrale 26r*
Closed Sunday. Hearty food and fun.

**Il Vecchio Vinaio**
*Via de'Neri 65r*
Closed Monday.

**Procacci**
*Via de' Tornabuoni 64r*
The place for wine and truffle sandwiches.

# Shopping

**I**n Florence, art has been closely linked to craftsmanship since Dante's time. From the former guilds of the *Arti e Mestieri* and the manufacturies of the former Grand Duchy right up to the present, the *botteghe* (once a 'school', now a 'shop') has always shown a high degree of creativity.

Naturally, not everything touted as *artigianato fiorentino* actually reflects this centuries-old culture and tradition. But, unlike almost any other city, Florence is the product of its mercantile capabilities and craftsmanship.

### Tuscan Products

Characteristic Tuscan products are leather goods and objects crafted from straw and cloth. Ever since the Middle Ages tanning and leather processing have played an important rôle here. At the addresses listed below you can still acquire top craftsmanship – although not always for small sums of money.

You can buy leather and straw products at the **Mercato Nuovo**. For exceptional silks pay a visit to Marchese Pucci's **Antico Setificio Fiorentino** (Via Bartolini 4, San Frediano). At **Sylvia's** (Via dei Tavolini 10) you will find a tremendous selection of trimmings and bordering materials. **Lisio** (Via dei Fossi, 45r) sells luxury fabrics.

At **Pineider's** on Via Tornabuoni 76r you will find stationary supplies – they hardly come any finer! **Giannini** (Piazza Pitti 37r)

also has a lot to offer: handbags and cases or bound books and notepads using the marbled paper. **Manelli Cellerini** on Via Santo Spirito makes hand-decorated cases and jewellery boxes. Handmade leather goods are also sold at **Il Bisonte** (Via del Parione 31r).

Even back in the guild era, the goldsmiths, silversmiths and jewellers played an important role: the Ponte Vecchio with its small shops is ample proof of this. Another interesting address is **Casa dell'Orafo** (next to Santo Stefano Church). If you want to meet the successors

of the Old Masters of jewellery, stop in at **Mario Buccellati**'s (Via Tornabuoni 71r), **Settepassi Faraone** (Via Tornabuoni 25r) or **Brandimarte** (Via Bertolini 18) – to name but a few.

You would be hard put to find the following craftsmen and restorers on your own. For woodcarvings and such, you can turn to **Bartolozzi e Maioli** (Via Maggio 13). For something unique try **Ficalli e Belloni** (Via delle Caldaie 25), who produce *trompe-l'oeil* pieces in wood or stone. In the **Emporio S.Firenze** (Piazza S Firenze 9r) you can buy cast-iron objects. For something a bit easier to carry, why don't you try **Emilio Paoli's** (Via della Vigna Nuova 26r), selling cane and straw objects. At **Paolo Pagliai's** (Borgo San Jacopo 41) you can have antique silver renovated or copied or order a set of table silver.

If you want something less 'cheap' to take home, I recommend the following Florentine antique dealers – but be prepared for reproductions as well as genuine antiques: **Guido Bartolozzi** (Via Maggio 18r), **Giovanni Pratesi** (Via Maggio 13) who specialises in the 17th century, **Alessandro Campolmi** (Via Magggio 5/ Sdrucciolo dei Pitti 22), **Giorgio Albertosi** (Piazza Frescobaldi 1r) who specialises in the 18th century, **Bellini** (Lungarno Soderini 5) as well as the auction house of Casa d'Aste Pitti (Via Maggio 15, tel: 055-2396382). There are also many antique shops on Via de'Fossi and on Borgo Ognissanti.

Still looking for that extra-special souvenir of Florence? Look in the lovely old pharmacies: the **Farmacia Santa Maria Novella** (Via della Scala 16r) is worth a visit in itself for its frescoed interior and wonderful range of fragrant soaps, toilet waters and pot pourri. You can also try **Antica Farmacia di San Marco** (Via Cavour, 146r), noted for colognes and medieval remedies, **Farmacia del Cinghiale** (in front of the Mercato Nuovo) or the **Profumeria Inglese** (Via Tornabuoni 97r).

## Books

The best places to go for books (in various languages) are **Feltrinelli** (Via Cavour 12) or **Seeber Messaggerie** (Via Tornabuoni 70r). The **Libreria Il Viaggio** (Via Ghibellina 117r) has the best selection of travel literature, maps and travel guides. For art books, try the **Libreria Salimbeni** (Via Palmieri 14–16r); for music books: **Il Fiorino della G.P.L.** (Via del Corso 43r). For a wide selection of books in English try the **Paperback Exchange** (Via Fiesolana 31r)

## Hairdressers

While you are in the fashion metropolis of Florence why not try a new look at **I Polverini** (Piazza Strozzi 4, tel: 055-287354) or **G. Marroncini** (Via della Vigna Nuova 22r, tel: 055-294813).

## Contact Lenses / Spectacles

If you want to be seen you need good (fore)sight: **Piancastelli** (Via Porta Rossa 48r, Phone: 055-210121) **L'occhialaio di Firenze** (Via dei Pucci 24r, tel: 055-2398663), **Ottica Fusi e Poggiali** (Via Roma 24r, tel: 055-292235) are all opticians with top selections in quite central locations.

## Couture

Nothing left to wear? This embarassing situation requires an immediate remedy. The first stop: **Gucci** (Via Tornabuoni 74r). Too conventional? How about shoes by **Ferragamo** (Via Tornabuoni 12r): they will not pinch your feet (almost as delightful as Birkenstock, but what a look!) – but maybe you are thinking of your wallet. **Luisa** (Via Roma 19r) has great things. Or how about **Valentino** (Via della Vigna Nuova 47r) or **Armani** (Via della Vigna Nuova 51) or the cheaper **Emporio Armani** (Piazza Strozzi 14–16r)? Having exclusive taste has always been a bit expensive. You could try **Principi** (Via degli Strozzi 21r) instead. They have everything from underpants to gloves. Or would you like to try **Emilio Pucci** (Via dei Pucci 6 and Via della Vigna Nuova 97) on for size? Prefer classic couture? **Neuber** is on Via Strozzi 32. Something traditional? Then **Old England** (Via Vecchietti 28/2) is the place or **Ugolini** (Via Tornabuoni 20). Ladies, you can take your husbands to **Zanobetti's** (Via Calimala 20) and your sons (or boyfriends?) to **Gerard's** (Via Vacchereccia 18-20r). Something for the house? **Bruna Spadolini** (Lungarno Archibusieri 4r) stocks tableclothes and sheets of real linen. A silk nightgown to go with them? Then pop around to **Loretta Caponi's** (Borgo Ognissanti 12r and Lungarno Vespucci 12r).

## Fine Foods

**Procacci** (Via Tornabuoni 64r) promises to please even the most demanding palates. Besides their famous *panini tartufati*, try the paté, all sorts of jams, tea, salamis etc, etc… **Pegna** (Via dello Studio 8) also has a wide selection in this category. You should also look around the **Mercato Centrale** (San Lorenzo).

## Markets

If you like browsing around, then you might try your luck among the stamps, antiques and (more or less) fascinating junk at the flea market on Piazza Ciompi. **S Ambrogio** (Piazza Lorenzo Ghiberti) is a food market, also offering new clothes and flowers. The **Mercato delle Cascine** (Tuesday) is the cheapest clothing market; food is also sold. The **Mercato di San Lorenzo** (new and used clothing) is an institution – not even recent political pressure could get rid of it. The **Mercato Centrale** (Via dell'Ariento, in the San Lorenzo quarter) is the largest food market. **The Mercato Nuovo** (*see page 24*) is the most touristy market.

## Gifts for Hosts

Here, as all over the world, it is customary to bring along flowers, wine or chocolates when invited to someone else's home. Some good addresses to know in Florence are: **Mercatelli** (Via del Parione 33) for flowers, the **Enoteca Pinchiorri** (Via Ghibellina 87) and the aristocratic wine estate, **Marchesi de' Frescobaldi** (Via di Santo Spirito) with the largest selection of bottles; and **Rivoire** (Piazza della Signoria) for the best in homemade chocolates.

## Hats / Suitcases and Leather Goods

After your shopping spree you are going to need a new suitcase: **Borsalino** (Via de Cimatori) and **Bojola** (Via Randinelli 25r, corner of Via de Banchi) have a large array of fine leather suitcases and hats. For something smarter, have a look at the selection at **Mandarina Duck** (Via Por Santa Maria). Exclusive handbags and gloves are on sale at **Cellerini** (Via del Sole 37r). Leather goods are also available from the reliable store **Raspini** (Via Roma 25r and Via Martelli 5r). It is also fun to visit the **Santa Croce**

**leather school** in part of the Santa Croce cloisters.

## Records / CDs

If you are interested in musical instruments, pianos, hi-fi, TVs, video equipment, musical books, etc, you will marvel at the extraordinary range of products at **Ricordi** (Via Brunelleschi 8r). For more modern merchandise such as CDs, try **Alberti** (Via dei Pucci 10–20r) and Borgo San Lorenzo with its terrific selection of records.

## Cleaners

You're in a sticky predicament: with breakfast marmalade on your new shirt and no fresh change of clothes. That's quite a jam! The **Lavanderia Lavaget** (Piazza Ghiberti) or the **Tintoria Fiorentina** (Via Palmieri 5r) may help you get your act cleaned up.

## Paraphernalia and Second Hand

At **Babilonia** (Piazza Mercato Centrale 37r) you'll need an entire afternoon to dig through everything! **Atelier Alice** (Via Faenza 12) stocks fanciful carnival masks. For antique toys and games visit **Antica Meraviglia** (Borgo San Jacopo).

## Sporting Goods

For sports kits and equipment, you can walk (or run) to either **Lo Sport** (Piazza Duomo 7–8r) or **Galleria dello Sport** (Via Ricasoli 25r). **Il Rifugio Sport** (Piazza Ottaviani 3r) is only a short distance from the centre of town. For standard sportswear and swimwear try Florence's two main department stores: **Coin** (Via dei Calzaiuoli 56r) and **UPIM** (Piazza della Repubblica).

# Practical Information

## TRAVEL ESSENTIALS

### When to Visit

Tuscany is worth a visit in any season. However, since the region goes through many changes throughout the year, your choice of season depends on which Tuscany you would like to see. If your main interest is in art and architecture, you should avoid August when many museums and institutions are closed.

If your plans focus on close contact with nature, you should avoid the months November to February because of frequent rain, as well as August because of the flood of tourists – unless you stick to smaller towns and the more remote regions (Garfagnana and Casentino, for example).

The Tuscan hot springs are ideal in late autumn, winter and the beginning of spring. The sea itself is enjoyable from April to late September, but thrashing around in milling crowds in August is not my idea of swimming.

Touring the main attractions of Florence, Siena and Pisa around Easter is nothing but torture. If you prefer a bit of everything – ie art, sea and countryside – I recommend May and June – or at least before 15 July when all the hustle and bustle starts. September and October are good months again, only expect a few rainy days.

### Visa Requirements

Citizens of the European Union countries require no visa. Other nationals only do so if they intend to stay longer than three months.

### Airports

**PERETOLA** (6km/4 miles from Florence) Via del Termine 1, tel: 055-373498
**GALLILEO GALLILEI** (international) Pisa, tel: 050-500707/050-216073.

## MONEY MATTERS

**First:** beware of the many zeroes (on the bills)!

**Second:** in the larger cities there are pickpockets.

**Third:** the lingering Italian recession and devaluation of the lire make Tuscany an appealing destination. Petrol costs around 1,600 lire per litre; the bill for an average meal is about 35,000 to 40,000 lire per person. In the cities a double room can hardly be had for less than 100,000 lire per night.

**Fourth:** in the morning banks have normal business hours (Monday to Friday 8.30am–1pm), in the afternoon most are open from 3–3.45pm. In large cities there are automatic exchange tellers; only in emergencies, however, are these worth the trouble, due to the adverse rates of exchange.

### Geography and Economy

Tuscany, with an area of 60,000 square miles (22,992km²) is the fifth largest region in Italy and has the shape of a triangle. Its northern border are the Apennines, the western boundary the Tyrrhenian Sea; in the south the complicated border is formed by mountain ridges, basins and plains.

Tuscany has nine provinces, 287 municipalities, a population of 3,568,799 with a density of 60 per square mile (155 per km²). The coastal strip from Carrara to Livorno and the lower Arno Valley from Florence to Pisa are densely populated. With the exception of the interior comprising the Maremma, the Campagna around Siena and the upper Apennines, the standard of living is a little higher than the national average.

Agriculture plays an important role, especially wine and olive-growing in the Chianti region and the cultivation of grain and vegetables in the Maremma. Cattle are raised mainly in the Maremma. Industrially, mining plays an important role. There is also significant metallurgy in Piombino, Livorno, Florence and San Giovanni Valdarno – with chemical plants polluting Rosignano and Livorno. Leather is tanned in Santa Croce on the Arno, glass is blown in Empoli and small trades flourish everywhere.

### Climate

One expects a Mediterranean climate – but these days nobody really knows what kind of weather to expect. In the last few years, spring has arrived much too early; then it wouldn't really turn into summer; then, in August, the temperatures would soar to 40°c/114°f making it unbearable, even in the water. After that not a drop of rain fell until November, and winter never got as cold as it should.

So: pack everything from swimming trunks to a raincoat – except a fur coat, which one does not need here (for climatic reasons, at least – they are *de rigueur* at theatres and opera where matrons would feel a chill without one – even in May at the Maggio Musicale Fiorentino).

### Time

Italy observes Central European Time (CET) with summer time in effect from the end of April through to the end of October.



### Car, Train or Bus?

The car is the most comfortable means of transport for individual travel, but also the most expensive – especially with petrol prices at such a high level in Italy (see: 'Money Matters').

Bus and train require more time. Trains are usually so overcrowded one seldom finds a seat – unless one takes special trains like the Intercity, Pendolino, etc. They, on the other hand, are considerably more expensive and do not stop at every town. The bus is an alternative to the car. Here are the addresses of the main bus companies:

Lazzi: Piazza Stazione 4-6r, Florence, phone: 055-215154
Sita: Via S Caterina da Siena 15r, tel: 055-483651
COPIT: Piazza S Maria Novella, Florence, tel: 055-215451
CAT: Via Fiume 2r, Florence, tel: 055-283400/283734
CAP: Piazza Stazione-Via Nazionale 13r, Florence, tele: 055-214637

In Florence you do not need a car at all. It is best to leave it in the hotel car park or park it at the Fortezza da Basso. The car-free zone is nearly as large as the historical part of the city itself – ie the entire area within the Viali di Circonvallazione ring is only open to buses, taxis and residential traffic. In the inner city there is a chronic parking problem. Besides, the centre of town is so small that it is much better to tour it on foot. The situation in other cities such as Pisa, Lucca or Siena is the same as in Florence. By parking the car outside the centre of town you will avoid a major headache. In selecting the routes for our tours we have avoided all highways and *superstrade*, intentionally picking side roads which will allow you actually to see what you have come here for.

## Maps

City maps are available at all kiosks and book stores; road maps and travel guides at specialist book stores, such as the **Libreria Il Viaggio**, Via Ghibellina, Florence.

## Sightseeing Tours

For information and reservations, contact any of the local tourist agencies listed under 'Travel Agents' in this guide (see *page 122*).

## Public Transportation

There is no metro in Florence, because the Etruscans and Romans would roll over in their graves, and the tramway has already 'bitten the dust'. The orange **ATAF** buses are still alive (Piazza della Stazione, tel: 055-580528). Buy the tickets either at a kiosk or in a *bar tabacchi* before boarding the bus. You can buy tickets valid for an hour, two hours or 24 hours.

If you are planning to stay more than a couple of days in Florence, consider getting a '*carta arancio*', a seven-day pass valid for all buses and trains in the province of Florence. The most useful buses are: No 7 (to Fiesole), No 13 (to Piazzale Michelangelo), No 15 (a circular sightseeing tour of the city).

## Auto Breakdown Service

Assistenza Automobilistica ACI
Phone: 055-24861 or phone: 116
A car breakdown rescue service is free to foreign-registered cars.

## *Car Rental in Florence*

**AVIS**
*Borgo Ognissanti 128r*
*Tel: 055-213629*

**EUROPCAR**
*Borgo Ognissanti 53-55r*
*Tel: 055-2360072*

**HERTZ**
*Via Maso Finiguerra 33r*
*Tel: 055-2398205*

**ITALY BY CAR**
*Borgo Ognissanti 134r*
*Tel: 055-293021*

**MAGGIORE**
*Via Maso Finiguerra 11r*
*Tel: 055-210238*

## WHERE TO STAY

## Hotels in Florence

Our selection distinguishes three hotel categories and lists the price of a double room with breakfast. This price will also serve as to estimate the price of a single room. Hotels in other parts of Tuscany are listed at the end of the relevant itinerary. Hotel beds in the city centre tend to be in great demand, so book ahead.

## *Luxury Class*

**EXCELSIOR**
*Piazza Ognissanti 3*
*Tel: 055-264201*
Double: 590,000 lire
Exclusive hotel with roof garden and piano bar; beautiful central location on the River Arno.

**GRAND HOTEL**
*Piazza Ognissanti*
*Tel: 055-288781*
Double: 630,000 lire
Freshly renovated, lovely salon.

**REGENCY**
*Piazza d'Azeglio 3*
*Tel: 055-245247*
Double: 540,000 lire
On the quiet Piazza d'Azeglio, 5 minutes from the centre of town. Excellent Tuscan cuisine.

**GRAND HOTEL VILLA CORA**
*Viale Machiavelli 18*
*Tel: 055-2298451*
Double: 590,000 lire
19th-century villa with a beautiful 'rural' location at the end of Viale dei Colli.

**HELVETIA & BRISTOL**
*Via dei Pescioni 2*
*Tel: 055-287814*
Double: 547,000 lire
Freshly renovated, in a central location.

**VILLA SAN MICHELE**
*Via Doccia 4*
*Fiesole*
*Tel: 055-59451*
Double: 1200,000
Former Franciscan monastery built according to plans by Michelangelo. Famous for its panorama of the city.

## Expensive

**BERCHELLI**
*Lugarno Acciaiuoli 14*
*Tel: 055-264061*
Double: 370,000 lire
Occupies a renovated 14th-century palazzo; atmospheric, with view of the Arno.

**BERNINI PALACE**
*Piazza S Firenze 29*
*Tel: 055-288621*
Double: 380,000 lire

**BRUNELLESCHI**
*Piazza S Elisabetta 3*
*Tel: 055-562068*
Double: 390,000 lire
This unusual hotel occupies a tower dating back to the 6th century.

**DE LA VILLE**
*Piazza Antinori 1*
*Tel: 055-2381805*
Double: 390,000 lire

**GRAND HOTEL MINERVA**
*Piazza S Maria Novella 16*
*Tel: 055-284555*
Double: 365,000 lire

**KRAFT**
*Via Solferino 2*
*Tel: 055-284273*
Double: 390,000 lire
A terrace and roof garden are among this hotel's attractions.

**MONTEBELLO SPLENDID**
*Via Montebello 60*
*Tel: 055-2398051*
Double: 365,000 lire
Elegant, classical villa.

**PLAZA HOTEL LUCCHESI**
*Lungarno della Zecca Vecchia 38*
*Tel: 055-264141*
Double: 390,000 lire
Historic house on the Arno.

**TORRE DI BELLOSGUARDO**
*Via Roti Michelozzi 2*
*Tel: 055-2298145*
Double: 330,000 lire
This quiet old castle with its few rooms affords a view of the entire city from a very special perspective.

## Moderate

**ANNALENA**
*Via Romana 34*
*Tel: 055-222402*
Double: 180,000 lire
Set in former convent.

**BEACCI TORNABUONI**
*Via Tornabuoni 3*
*Tel: 055-212645*
Double: 250,000 lire
Set in medieval palazzo.

**LOGGIATO DEI SERVITI**
*Piazza SS Annunziata 3*
*Tel: 055-289592*
Double: 225,500 lire
Every room has antique furniture.

QUISISANA E PONTE VECCHIO
*Lungarno Archibusieri 4*
*Tel: 055-216692*
Double: 180,000 lire
Location for James Ivory's film *Room
with a View*.

PORTA ROSSA
*Via Porta Rossa 19*
*Tel: 055-287551*
Double: 180,000
Very centrally located; antique atmo-
sphere in spacious palazzo.

VILLA LE RONDINI
*Via Bolognese Vecchia 224*
*Tel: 055-400081*
Double: 230,000 lire
Set in olive groves 7km (4 miles) from
Florence. Tennis and swimming.

VILLA BELVEDERE
*Via Benedetto Castelli*
*Tel: 055-222501*
Double: 280,000 lire
Once belonged to the Medici.

CALZAIUOLI
*Via de'Calzaiuoli 6*
*Tel: 055-212456*
Double: 170,000 lire
Centrally located. Small but noble.

BENCISTA
*Via Benedetto da Maiano 4, Fiesole*
*Tel: 055-59163*
Double: 170,000 lire. Sprawling villa
in Fiesole, with rustic antiques.

CASA DEL LAGO
*Lungarno Vespucci 58*
*Tel: 055-216141*
Double: 110,000 lire

CONSIGLI
*Lungarno Vespucci 50*
*Tel: 055-214172*
Double: 150,000 lire

CROCINI
*Corso Italia 28*
*Tel: 055-212905*
Double: 115,000 lire

## Camp Sites

ITALIANI E STRANIERI
*Viale Michelangelo 80*
*Tel: 055-6531089*
320 tent sites
Closed November to March.

VILLA CAMERATA
*Viale Augusto Righi 2-4*
*Tel: 055-610300*
55 tent sites

## Youth Hostels

VILLA CAMERATA
*Viale A.Righi 2-4*
*Tel: 055-601451*
500 beds, April to September.
Beautiful 19th-century villa. Catch bus
No 170 from the station.

SANTA MONICA
*Via Santa Monica 6*
*Tel: 055-268338*
13 rooms, 111 beds. Book well ahead
for all budget accommodation.

## HEALTH & EMERGENCIES

**SOS: Emergency Numbers**
Central SOS: 113
Police: 112
Fire department: 115
Ambulances (Florence) 212222
Pharmacies/Information: 192

Car breakdown service: 116

**24-hour Pharmacy**
COMUNALE NO 13
*Interno Stazione S Maria Novella*
*Tel: 055-216761*

**Medical Emergencies**
All of Tuscany, tel: 118

**Tourist Medical Centre, Florence**
*Via Lorenzo il Magnifico 59*
*Tel: 055-475411*
Call this service first – it has multilingual doctors on 24-hour call.

**Associazione Volontari Ospedalieri, Florence:**
*Tel: 055-403126*
**Siena:**
*Tel: 0577-299362*
This free service offer interpreters to help in health matters.

**Florence Hospital**
*Santa Maria Nuova*
*Piazza di Santa Maria Nuova*
*Tel: 055-27581*

**Siena Hospital**
*Presidio Ospedaliero Santa Maria della Scala*
*Piazza del Duomo*
*Tel: 0577-299111*

**Pisa Hospital**
*Via Roma 67*
*Tel: 050-592111*



Shops are open in summer: 9am–1pm, 4–8pm; in winter: 9am–1pm, 3.30–7.30pm. All grocery stores are closed Wednesday afternoon.

### Holidays

| | |
|---|---|
| **New Year's Day:** | 1 January |
| **Epiphany:** | 6 January |
| **Shrove Tuesday** | |
| **Good Friday** | |
| **Easter Monday** | |
| **Liberation Day:** | 25 April |
| **May Day:** | 1 May |
| **Ascension Day** | |
| **Whit Monday** | |
| **Corpus Christi** | |
| **Proclamation of the Republic:** | 2 June |
| **Assumption of the Virgin Mary (Ferragosto):** | 15 August |
| **All Saints' Day:** | 1 November |
| **Italian Union Day:** | 4 November |
| **Festa della Madonna:** | 8 December |
| **Christmas Day:** | 25 December |
| **Santo Stefano:** | 26 December |



### Post and Telephone

**Hours of Business:** 8.15am–2.40pm; Saturday 8.15–noon; closed Sunday and holidays.

**Main Office: Palazzo delle Poste**
Via Pellicceria. 8.15am–7pm for all services. The best place to make long-distance calls: open around the clock for telephoning. In the street, up-to-date pay phones accept telephone cards (*carta* or *scheda telefonica*). These can be bought from kiosks or tobacconists (*tabacchi*), or from wherever a large 'T' sign is displayed.

To dial other countries first dial the international access code 00, then the country code: Australia (61); France (33); Germany (49); Japan (81); Netherlands (31); Spain (34); UK (44); US and Canada (1). If using a US credit phone card, dial the company's access number: Sprint, Tel: 172 1877; AT&T, Tel: 172 1011; MCI, Tel: 172 1022.

### Radio and Television

*Raiuno, Raidue* and *Raitre* are the state-run stations.

Other important stations are *Canale 5, Rete 4* and *Italia 1* – all owned by

Silvio Berlusconi, recent premier and media mogul.

The real Tuscan stations are: *Teleregione, Tele Libera Firenze, Rete A, Canale 10,* and *Video Firenze.* Each one worse than the last.

*Radio Montebeni* (108FM) plays only classical music. The most listened-to radio stations are: *Lady Radio, Radio Cuore* and *Crudelia* – and the names speak for themselves!

### Newspapers

The newsstands carry the following: *La Nazione, La Repubblica, Il Tirreno, L'Unità, Firenze La Sera* and *Firenze Spettacolo* are good listings magazines (and easy to understand). *Events in Florence and Tuscany* is just that.

The Tuscan newspaper per se is the conservative *La Nazione.* The more progressive *La Repubblica* is actually a nationally circulated newspaper with a detailed local supplement. *Il Tirreno* is distributed mainly along the coast. *Firenze La Sera* and *Firenze Spettacolo* provide information about events.

## CALENDAR OF EVENTS

**JANUARY:** Pitti Uomo, Pitti Bimbo – Fashion Week in Florence.

**FEBRUARY/MARCH:** Carnivals in Viareggio, Arezzo and San Gimignano.

**MARCH:** Easter Sunday festival held in Florence.

**APRIL/MAY:** Arts and Crafts Fair.

**MAY/JUNE:** Maggio Musicale Fiorentino, opera, ballet and concerts. For premieres reserve well in advance.

**24** and **28 JUNE:** Calcio in Costume, football game in medieval costume.

**24 JUNE:** S Giovanni, the patron saint of Florence; fireworks. One of the most important public festivals.

**7 SEPTEMBER:** *Rificolona:* lantern procession in Florence.

**SEPTEMBER/OCTOBER:** Wine and food fairs in the Chianti; saracen tournament in Arezzo (first Sunday in September). Feast of Santa Croce in Lucca (13–14 September).

**NOVEMBER:** Feast of Santa Cecilia in Siena (22 November)

## NIGHTLIFE

Florence is not New York, and there is not much of a disco scene – especially since most places close quite early. During the last few years there has been as much quarrelling over closing times as over the pedestrian precinct. Many discos are outside town, because concessions are no longer issued for the centre.

### Discotheques and Nightclubs

**TROPICANA AT CENTRAL PARK**
*Via del Fosso Macinante 2–4*
*Tel: 055-333488*
Outdoor discotheque in the Cascine park. Opens at 10pm.

**MANILA**
*Piazza Matteucci*
*Campi Bisenzio*
*Tel: 055-894121*
Live music; popular in avant garde circles. Friday to Sunday only, at 10pm.

**FANDANGO**
*Via dell'Erta Canina 12*
*Tel: 055-2343903*
Opens at 10pm. Predominantly young.

### JACKIE O

*Via dell'Erta Canina 24b*
*Tel: 055-234244*
This is a posh nightclub for a thirty-something crowd who have made it to the top.

### ROCKCAFÉ

*Borgo degli Albizi 66r*
*Tel: 055-244662*
Opens at 10pm. This is the only rock disco in town. Reguarly stages live concerts.

### YAB YUM

*Via dei Sassetti 5r*
*Tel: 055-282018*
Opens at 11pm nightly; closed Sunday and Monday. Right downtown. Droves of in-crowders.

### TENAX

*Via Pratese 46a*
*Tel: 055-308160*
Opens at 10pm Wednesday to Saturday. A popular multimedia meeting place favoured by the artistic and musical avant-garde.

### SPACE ELECTRONIC

*Via Palazzuolo 37*
*Tel: 055-293082*
Opens at 9.30 p.m. Space Electronic is the largest teenage-oriented disco in Florence with special effects, lasers, spaceships.

### MARAMAO

*Via de' Macci 79r*
*Tel: 055-2444341*
Opens at midnight on Thursday and Saturday only.

## Bars

There are numerous bars. Here is a selection of the most distinctive.

### CAFFE

*Piazza Pitti 9*
*Tel: 055-296241*
Closed Monday. Exclusive; furnished with antiques and sofas – ideal for a quiet evening.

### LA DOLCE VITA

*Piazza del Carmine*
*Tel: 055-284595;*
10pm–1am; closed Sunday.
In summer this is one of the most heavily frequented bars in Florence: a place for jazz, blues and live music in general. Very 'in' among those who want to be seen. If you cannot get in – which is usually the case – you take a seat on the roof of a parked car to enjoy the beautiful setting of the Piazza.

### ROSE'S

*Via del Parione 26r*
*Tel: 055-287090*
Closed Sunday.
Always full. Plenty of cocktails and long drinks. Also good for snack lunch.

### CAFFÉ CIBREO

*Via del Verrocchio 5r*
*Tel: 055-2341100*
Closed Sunday and Monday.
Next to Cibreo restaurant.Quiet and refined. Very sophisticated.

### CAFFE VOLTAIRE

*Via della Scala 9r*
*Tel: 055-218255*
8am–4pm; Sunday 5pm–4am.
Frequently interesting programmes.

Former Sixties crowd watering hole. Now a private club: inexpensive membership required.

## BLOB
*Via Vinegia 21*
*Tel: 055-290926*
Set behind the Palazzo Vecchio, this is a good place for live music – jazz, Latin or piano music.

## ART BAR
*Via del Moro 4r*
*Tel: 055-287661*
Very small – extremely popular among foreign students.

## MONTECARLA CLUB
*Via dei Bardi 2*
*Tel: 055-2340259*
Amusing kitsch.

### Traditional Bars and Caffès

## PASZKOWSKI
*Piazza della Repubblica 6*
*Tel: 055-2398206*
Closed Monday.
An institution. Open until 1.30am. Evergreens on the piano. Elderly ladies have a great time here.

## GILLI
*Piazza della Repubblica 39r*
*Tel: 055-2396310*
Closed Tuesday. Sit and watch the people stroll by – preferably in the first spring sunshine.

## GIACOSA
*Via Tornabuoni 83r*
*Tel: 055-2396226*
Closed Sunday. At noon the businessmen and lawyers meet for a hasty bite to eat.

## RIVOIRE
*Piazza della Signoria 5r*
*Tel: 055-214412*
Closed Monday, as well as the second half of January. Sitting in the sun, taking in the Piazza. Otherwise you cannot say you have been to Florence.

## GIUBBE ROSSE
*Piazza della Repubblica 13r*
*Tel: 055-212280*
Closed Wednesday.
Historical bar – once the haunt of artists and intellectuals.

## PROCACCI
*Via Tornabuoni 64r*
*Tel: 055-211656*
Same hours of business as the shops. A truffle sandwich is simply *bon ton*!

## CAFFE DONEY
*Piazza Strozzi 18*
*Tel: 055-2398206*
Fashionable haunt.

## CAFFELLATTE
*Via degli Alfani 93r*
*Tel: 055-2478878*
8am–1.30pm, 3.30–7.30pm.
Closed Sunday. Warm rolls, cakes, granola, tea in all variations, etc.

### Live Music

Before setting out, pick up a copy of *Firenze Spettacolo*, the main city listings magazine. Most music clubs are closed on Monday; very few get going before 10pm.

## CHIODO FISSO
*Via Dante Alighieri 16r*
*Tel: 055-2381290*
Long-established wine and guitar bar.
Owner and bard in one person.

## JAZZ CLUB
*Via Nuova dei Caccini 3*
*Tel: 055-2479700*
The oldest jazz joint in town. Beer.

## RIFLISSI D'EPOCA
*Via dei Renai 13r*
*Tel: 055-2342622*
Opens at 10pm and has the longest
hours in town. Continuous turnover:
the audience changes as the night
progresses.

## FLORG CONCERTI
*Via Michele Mercati 24*
*Tel: 055-490437*
The place for rock, including alternative
bands. Open Thursday to Sunday sum-
mer only; bus No 4.

### Florentine Museums and Churches

## PITTI PALACE
*Piazza Pitti*
*Tel: 055-210323*
All museums within the Pitti (the Galleria d'Arte Moderna, Galleria Palatina,
Museo Degli Argenti, Museo delle Por-
cellane) are open 9am–2pm (9am–1pm
on Sunday). The adjoining Boboli Gardens (open 9am to one hour before sunset) are also worth the high separate
admission charge.

## MEDICI CHAPELS (CAPPELLE MEDICEE)
*Piazza Madonna degli Aldobrandini*
*Tel: 055-213206*
9am–2pm; Sunday and holidays 9am–
1pm; closed Monday.

## CENACOLO DEL GHIRLANDAIO
*Borgo Ognissanti 42*
*Tel: 055-296802*
Only open Monday, Tuesday and Sat-
urday 9am–noon.
Free admission.

## CHIOSTRO DELLO SCALZO
*Via Cavour 69*
*Tel: 055-472812*
Only open Monday and Thursday
9am–1pm.
Free admission to this frescoed cloister
by San Marco.

## CROCIFISSIONE DEL PERUGINO
*Borgo Pinti 58*
9–noon, 5–7pm.
Phone: 055-2478420

## GALLERIA DELL'ACCADEMIA
*Via Ricasoli 60*
*Tel: 055-214375*
9am–7pm; Sunday and holidays 9am–
2pm; closed Monday.
Houses the celebrated *David*.

## CAPPELLA BRANCACCI
*Piazza del Carmine*
Open 7am–noon and 3–7pm.
The expensive admission charge to the
Cappella Brancacci is worth it to see
the great works by Masaccio and Ma-
solini. However, in summer or if
crowded, visits are limited to just 15
minutes.

**DUOMO (FLORENCE CATHEDRAL)**
*Santa Maria del Fiore*
*Piazza del Duomo*
For the differing opening times of the different sections of the cathedral (such as dome, crypt, belltower and Museo dell'Opera del Duomo) see Tour 1 (*pages 20–25*).

**GALLERIA DEGLI UFFIZI**
*Loggiato degli Uffizi 6*
*Tel: 055-218341*
9am–7pm; Sunday and holidays 9am–1pm; closed Monday.

**GIARDINO DI BOBOLI**
*Piazza Pitti*
*Tel: 055-213440*
Open 9am–one hour before sunset.

**MUSEO ARCHEOLOGICO**
*Via della Colonna 36*
*Tel: 055-2478641*
9am–2pm; Sunday and holidays 9am–1pm; closed Monday.

**MUSEO DELLA CASA FIORENTINA ANTICA**
*Palazzo Davanzati*
*Via Porta Rossa 13*
*Tel: 055-216518*
9am–2pm; Sunday and holidays 8am–1pm. Closed Monday.
An enchanting museum of Florentine artefacts occupying an historic palazzo.

**MUSEO NAZIONALE DEL BARGELLO**
*Via del Proconsolo 4*
*Tel: 055-210801*
9am–2pm; Sunday and holidays 9am–1pm; closed Mondays.
Works by Michelangelo and Donatello – magnificent sculpture.

**MUSEO DI SAN MARCO**
*Piazza San Marco 1*
*Tel: 055-210741*
9am–2pm; Sunday and holidays 9am–1pm; closed Monday.
Splendidly frescoed monastery.

**MUSEO 'FIRENZE COM'ERA'**
*Via dell'Oriuolo 24*
*Tel: 055-298483*
10am–1pm; Sunday and holidays 8am–1pm; closed Thursday.

**GALLERIA DELLO SPEDALE DEGLI INNOCENTI**
*Piazza SS Annunziata 12*
*Tel: 055-243670*
9am–2pm; Sunday and holidays 8am–1pm; closed Wednesday.
Small museum on Renaissance square.

**MUSEO S MARIA NOVELLA**
*Piazza S Maria Novella*
*Tel: 055-282187*
9am–2pm; Sunday and holidays 8am–1pm; closed Friday.

**PALAZZO VECCHIO**
*Piazza della Signoria*
*Tel: 055-2768465*
9am–7pm; Sunday and holidays 8am–1pm.

**MUSEO DI STORIA DELLA SCIENZA**
*Piazza de'Giudici 1*
*Tel: 055-293493*
Monday to Saturday 9.30am–1pm; Monday, Wednesday and Friday also 2–5pm; closed Sunday and holidays.

MUSEO ZOOLOGICO 'LA SPECOLA'
*Via Romana 17*
*Tel: 055-222451*
Monday, Tuesday, Thursday, Friday and Saturday 9am–noon.

ORTO BOTANICO 'GIARDINO DEI SEMPLICI' (BOTANIC GARDENS)
*Via Micheli 3*
Monday, Wednesday and Friday 9am–noon, tel: 055-284696. Free admission.

SANTO SPIRITO
*Piazza Santa Spirito*
Church open 8am–noon and 4–6pm.

## Theatre

Florence hosts a major classical music event, the annual Maggio Musicale Fiorentino. It is held between late May and July in some of the following venues, as well as in Fiesole.

Ask at the tourist office for information about these and other theatre and music events (Chiasso Baroncelli 17r, tel: 055-2302124 or 2302033 – situated in an alley behind the Palazzo Vecchio).

TEATRO COMUNALE
*Corso Italia 12*
*Tel: 055-2779236*

TEATRO DELLA PERGOLA
*Via della Pergola 12-32*
*Tel: 055-2479651*

TEATRO NICCOLINI
*Via Ricasoli 5*
*Tel: 055-2398333*

TEATRO VERDI
*Via Ghibellina 99*
*Tel: 055-2396242*

## Ticket Sales

BOX OFFICE
*Via Faenza 139r*
*Tel: 055-210804*

AGENZIA GLOBUS
*Piazza Santa Trinita 2r*
*Tel: 055-214992*

## SPORT

**Golf**
GOLF DELL'UGOLINO
*Via Chiantigiana 3*
*Impruneta (18km from Florence)*
*Tel: 055-2051155*

**Tennis**
The Cascine park has a tennis club open to the general public.
*Tel: 055-356651*

**Swimming**
The Piscina le Pavoniere in the Cascine park (open summer 10am–6pm) is the nicest public pool in Florence. Also try the Piscina Comunale on Lungarno Colombo 6.

**Riding**
CENTRO IPPICO TOSCANO 'LE CASCINE'
*Via Vespucci 5a*
*Tel: 055-372621*

Expect to wait a ridiculously long time to be served in banks, even for simple transactions like changing currency. Any banks displaying a *cambio* sign will change foreign currency or traveller's cheques.

Foreign exchange kiosks (*see below*) are generally quicker and are open longer than banks but usually offer poorer rates of exchange. Banks are in great supply, however, and usually open from 8.30am– 1pm Monday to Friday; some are open in the afternoons for 2.30–4pm.

### Banks

**BANCA NAZIONALE DEL LAVORO**
*Via Strozzi 1*

**BANCA TOSCANA**
*Via Panclado 4*

**CASSA DI RISPARMIO DI FIRENZE**
*Via Bufalini 4*

**BANCA COMMERCIALE ITALIANA**
*Via Strozzi 8*

### Exchange Kiosks

**EXACT**
*Via dei Calzaiuoli 42*
*Via Por Santa Maria 3r*
*Via Alamanni 93*
These are usueful places to exchange money outside normal banking hours. You can also try the exchange facility in the railway station.

### Travel Agencies

**AIRLINES BOOKING CENTER**
*Via dei Banchi 23-27r*
*Tel: 055-473493*
**AMERICAN EXPRESS COMPANY**
*Via Guicciardini 49r*
*Tel: 055-288751*

*Via Dante Alighieri 14*
*Tel: 055-50981*

**CIT (COMPAGNIA ITALIANA TURISMO)**
*Via Cavour 56r*
*Tel: 055-294306*
*Piazza Stazione 51r*
*Tel: 055-284145*

**WORLD VISION TRAVEL**
In Florence:
*Lungarno degli Acciauoli 4*
*Tel: 055-295271*
In Pisa:
*Piazza della Repubblicca 3*
*Tel: 050-581014*



### Tourist Information

The annual *Pagine Gialle per il Turismo* contain a convenient compilation of addresses and telephone numbers of institutions which are of particular interest to tourists.

Either *Pro Loco* or the *Azienda Autonoma del Turismo* have offices in all the major towns in Tuscany – but they are not always very useful. Quite often the offices are closed or they have run out of up-to-date information material. On the other hand, you may strike lucky and meet some very nice and helpful people there.

Via Cavour 1r. Tel: 055-2760381/290832
Chiasso Baroncelli 17r. Tel: 055-2302124
Railway Station. Tel: 055-2381226/212245

## Lost & Found

**OGGETTI SMARRITI**
*Via Circondarioa 19*
*Tel: 055-367943*

**PARCO AUTO REQUISITE**
(pound for towed-away cars)
*Via Circondaria 19, Florence*
*Tel: 055-32831*
In Pisa: *Tel: 050-501444*
In Siena: *Tel: 0577-292550*

## Thermal Baths

**TERME DI FIRENZE**
*Fasciani-Impruneta (Firenze)*
*Cia Cassia 193*
April to October

**TERME DI BAGNOLO**
*Monterotondo Marittimo (Grosseto)*
*Tel: 0566-96633*

**TERME DI PETRIOLO**
*Petriolo (Grosseto)*
*Tel: 0564-908871*

**TERME SAN GIOVANNI**
*Saline-Porto Ferraio (Livorno)*
*Tel: 0565-92680*
20 April to 31 October

**TERME VALLE DEL SOLE**
*Via Aurelia Nord*
*Venturina-Caldana Terme*
*(Livorno)*
*Tel: 0586-51066*
April to November

**TERME DI BAGNI DI LUCCA**
*Bagni di Lucca (Lucca)*
*Tel: 0583-87223*

**TERME DI CASCIANA**
*Piazza Garibaldi 9*
*Casciana Terme (Pisa)*
*Tel: 0587-646112*
1 Apri to 30 November

**TERME DI S GUILIANO**
*Piazza Repubblica*
*S Guiliano Terme (Pisa)*
*Tel: 050-818047*

**TERME DI MONSUMMANO**
*Monsummano Terme (Pistoia)*
*Grotta Giusti*
*Tel: 0572-51008*
1 April to 20 November (Grotta Giusti)
16 May to 20 October (Grotta Parlanti)

**TERME DI MONTECATINI**
*Viale Verdi 41*
*Montecatini Terme (Pistoia)*
*Tel: 0572-75851*

**TERME DI CHIANCIANO**
*Viale Roma*
*Chianciano Terme (Siena)*
*Tel: 0578-63167*
16 April to 15 November

**TERME DI MONTEPULCIANO**
*Via delle Terme 46*
*Terme di Montepulciano (Siena)*
*Tel: 0578-79086*
16 April to 31 October

**TERME DI RAPOLANO**
*Rapolano Terme (Siena)*
*Tel: 0577-724030*
June to 20 October

**TERME DI S FILIPPO**
*Bagni di S Filippo (Siena)*
*Tel: 0577-872982*
1 June to 15 October

## For Children

The Cooperativa dei Ragazzi (Via San Gallo 27, Phone: 055-287500) has plenty of books (also in English and

French) and games for children of all ages. The staff are also glad to pass on information. There are sometimes activites in the afternoon

## LUDOTECA CENTRALE
*(Piazza SS Annunziata 13)*
*Tel for information: 055-2478386.*
Closed Wednesday as well as Saturday afternoon. A fun children's centre with activities for children under six.

## BABY-SITTING
*Via del Castellaccio 45r*
*Tel: 055-289382*

## PARK AND WALKS
In Florence, children enjoy the Boboli gardens, situated around the Pitti Palace, which are fun to clamber around (café on site too). The Cascine, Florence's other park, has a tiny zoo, which is popular with small children, not to mention a good swimming pool.

In the rest of Tuscany, popular children's facilities/activities include:

## PISTOIA ZOO
*Via Pieve a Celle, Pistoia*
*Tel: 0573-939219*
A well-designed place.

## PINOCCHIO PARK (Parcodi Pinocchio)
*Collodi*
*(near Pisa)*
*Tel: 0572-429342*
Open 8.30am–sunset.

## THE MAREMMA
*See Tour 2*
A good place for walks and willdlife spotting.

## Q, R



## S

# ACKNOWLEDGMENTS

| | |
|---|---|
| *49, 50, 51, 52, 53, 57, 58, 59, 60, 61* | **Silvia Brunelli** |
| *62, 65T, 69, 72T, 73, 75, 76, 89, 90, 92* | |
| *100, 101* | **Edizioni Ciao** |
| *99* | **Edizioni Novanta** |
| *5, 20, 22T, 24B, 25, 30, 31, 33, 38, 39B, 40,* | **Stefano Geraldi** |
| *41, 42, 43, 45, 46, 68, 71, 72B, 74, 77, 78,* | |
| *82, 86, 98, 104, 105, 106, 112–13* | |
| *24, 35* | **Frances Gransden** |
| *3, 54, 55, 63, 79, 87, 91, 107B,* | **Hans Jürgen Truöl** |
| *109, 110, 112, 115, 116, 123* | |
| *21, 22B, 23, 27, 28, 29, 34, 37, 39T, 47, 65B,* | **Bill Wassman** |
| *66, 67, 81, 83, 84, 85, 94, 95, 97, 103, 107T, 111* | |
| | |
| *Cover Design* | **Klaus Geisler** |
| *Handwriting* | **V Barl** |
| *Cartography* | **Berndtson & Berndtson** |